SCRATCH BEGINNINGS

ME, $25, AND THE SEARCH FOR THE AMERICAN DREAM

Adam Shepard

SB Press

500 North Street

Chapel Hill, NC 27514

www.scratchbeginnings.com

ISBN-13: 978-0-9796926-0-4

ISBN-10: 0-9796926-0-1

Library of Congress Catalog Number: 2007905879

Printed in the United States of America

*For Derrick, who knows
what he wants and goes for it.*

*And for BG and Omar,
who are almost there.*

Contents

ACKNOWLEDGMENTS

There are a number of people that deserve more than a simple "thanks" for their assistance in the writing of this book.

First shout-outs to Amy Brust and Nicki Jhabvala, who turned an amateurish first draft into a respectable second.

To the rest of my review crew, who should not by any means be discounted for being "the rest of my review crew:" Molly Beam, Angela Caira, Neil Cotiaux, Liz Duhamel, Sarah Haynes, Jen Golojuch, Timmy McAleer, Jaime-Lyn Pickles, Jan Richards, Surry Roberts, and Michael Thomas. A special thanks to Iain Levison and Fred Hobson—authors much more skilled than I will ever be—who kept me grounded.

To Teresa Pierrie, my ninth grade English teacher, who sparked a passion in writing that I may not have discovered on my own. And then showed me how to do it.

And, most importantly, to my parents—George and Joanie Shepard—who instilled in me the knowledge to conceive such a project and inspired me with the courage to complete it.

DISCLAIMER AND AUTHOR'S NOTES

Please be forewarned that my story does contain some profane language. I considered censoring the entire book in an effort to reach a wider audience, but, in the end, I decided it would take away from some of the people that I met along the way. Submerged in a world that used cursing as a form of expression, I wrote it like they said it, even toning it back somewhat with guys like Phil Coleman and Brooklyn Bonesy.

It is NOT recommended that the reader repeats the exact actions contained herein. By reading this book, the reader agrees to release the author, the publisher, the book seller, and all other interested parties from any liability stemming from events related to the contents of this book.

The truth is that I wouldn't wish my experience—especially the first 70 days—on anyone. Go to school, find your passion, save your money, live your dreams.

Finally, last names have been changed in order to protect the privacy of the people with whom I was associated throughout my year. Additionally, some of the names of the organizations with which I was associated have been changed.

JULY 24——SETTING UP

M y mom is nervous. My pops seems more excited about it than I am. My brother anxiously awaits my departure so he can take possession of my bed and all of my clothes after I leave.

My friend Sana is stimulated by curiosity, while Matt thinks I may have simply gone mad.

And maybe he is right. I am very frustrated.

I am frustrated with the whining and complaining.

Frustrated with the materialistic individualism that seems to be shaping every thirteen-year-old to be the next teen diva.

Frustrated with the lethargy and lack of drive.

Frustrated at always hearing how it "used to be" when people talk about the good ol' days in the same breath as their perceived demise of America.

I am really, really frustrated with the poor attitudes that seem to have swept over my peer group. Frustrated with hearing "I don't have" rather than "Let's see what I can do with what I do have."

So, I have decided to attempt to demonstrate that it doesn't have to be that way

There are many ways that I could go about this. I could work my way through years and years of school, and when the time came for me to write my dissertation, I could turn my teachings into a book perhaps worthy of being published that talked about the science of change or the science of attitude. I would write a comma and PhD next to my name on the cover and, based on my experience, people would know that whatever I had to say was inevitably true.

I could become the subject of a psychological case study on change that would highlight the importance of adopting a new way of thinking. I would find myself at the mercy of one of those aforementioned PhDs, hoping that he or she knew enough to use my talents—or lack thereof—productively.

Or, I can take matters into my own hands. And that's what I have decided to do. I have had the idea in my pocket, itching to come out, a plan that I have been toying with since high school. And now that I am fresh out of college, broke, and bordering on homelessness anyway, it seems like as good a time as any to let it out.

Here's my premise:

I am going to start almost literally from scratch with one 8' x 10' tarp, a sleeping bag, an empty gym bag, $25, and the clothes on my back. Via train, I will be dropped at a random place somewhere in the southeastern United States that is not in my home state of North Carolina. I have 365 days to become free of the realities of homelessness and become a "regular" member of society. After one year, for my project to be considered successful, I have to possess an operable automobile, live in a furnished apartment (alone or with a roommate), have $2,500 in cash, and, most importantly, I have to be in a position in which I can continue to improve my circumstances by either going to school or starting my own business.

There are a few ground rules that I need to establish in an effort to keep some critics at bay. On paper, my previous life doesn't exist for this one year. I cannot use any of my previous contacts, my college education, or my credit history. For the sake of this project, I have a high school diploma, and I will have recently moved to my new town. Additionally, I cannot beg for money or use services that others are not at liberty to use. Aside from illegally sleeping in a park or under a bridge, I am free to do whatever I need to do within the confines of the law in order to accomplish my goal.

Well, that all sounds simple enough. Now for a few disclaimers on my behalf.

First of all, I feel it is necessary to establish that I have no political affiliation—right wing, left wing, conservative, liberal, Republican, or Democrat. For the next year, they're all the same to me. Socioeconomically speaking, my story is a rebuttal to Barbara Ehrenreich's *Nickel and Dimed* and *Bait and Switch*, the books that spoke on the death of the American Dream. With investigative projects of her own, Ehrenreich attempted to establish that working stiffs are doomed to live in the same disgraceful conditions forever. I reject that theory, and my story is a search to evaluate if hard work and discipline provide any payoff whatsoever or if they are, as Ehrenreich suggests, futile pursuits.

Second, I am not an author or a journalist. I only mention this to establish that my intent in this project is not to produce a divine work of literature where carefully comprised prose seems to dance sublimely off the page. I'm just a regular guy, so whatever you read is straight from my thoughts to the paper. In a way, I believe that my untapped mind will add to the value of my writing. After all, I'm going into this without making any assumptions, which means unbiased reporting.

Third, it is important that I note that evaluators of this project are going to call me on all sorts of technicalities. Whether it be the absence of a family to tend to, as is the case for many in the real world living in similar circumstances, or my innate sense of adventure or my overall health that plays to my advantage—all are fair criticisms and worth noting. However, my hope is that these thoughts will not take away from the tedious task at hand or the theme that I intend to represent.

I also want to point out that I am not going to attempt to strengthen my story by flooding you with a wide range of statistics and information from books or magazines or other periodicals. While this is certainly a research project of sorts and there are points to be made, I feel it is important that I draw only from my own experience.

As you're going to see throughout the course of my journey, this is not a modern-day rags-to-riches, get-rich-quick story. "I made a million, and *you can too!*" Nope. That's too cliché, and, ironically, too unrealistic. Mine is the story of rags-to-fancier-rags. I'm not an extraordinary person performing extraordinary feats. I don't have some special talent that I can use to "wow" prospective employers. I'm average. My story is very basic, simple. My story is about the attitude of success. My goal is to better my lot and to provide a stepping-stone over the next 365 days for everything else I want to accomplish in my life. I aim to find out if the American Dream is still alive, or if it has, in fact, been drowned out by the greed of the upper class coupled with the apathy of the lower class.

So, here we go. You, my audience:

The dad who can use this book when his twelve-year-old is complaining about not having the latest video game.

The fifteen-year-old who doesn't quite understand why he or she has to study so hard and take "all of these worthless classes that I'll never use in real life."

The recent college grad who—drowned in student loans and limited opportunities (and, of course, living at home)—is searching for any little bit of strength and direction.

The seventy-two-year-old grandfather who already has a firm grasp on the concept of my story and has doubtless lived many of these same experiences.

The thirty-two-year-old mother of two who is working multiple jobs just to get by. The one making the sacrifice so her children can have a shot at the American Dream that she gave up on long ago.

You, the underdog, sitting behind the eight ball, wondering when your number is going to be called.

And me, with $25 and my personal belongings on my back, ready for the craziest adventure of my life ...

ONE

WELCOME TO CRISIS MINISTRIES

❧

There was nobody there.

There has always been somebody there to greet me. After every trip I've taken, it's either been Ma or Pops, a friend, a girlfriend, or, once, even a professor.

But not that night.

Nope. All that welcomed me was the humid evening air of Charleston, South Carolina, the rancid smell of urine leaking from the stalls of the train station's restrooms, and a scruffy looking man gripping a Styrofoam cup half full with coins. That night, I was greeted by a totally new world.

But that was to be expected. I had been preparing for the unpleasant insecurity of that first night ever since my brother had dropped me off earlier in the day at the Amtrak station in Raleigh on his way to work. I had been preparing for my first moment of freedom for far longer than I could remember.

There are plenty of ways to get from Raleigh to Charleston, the city that I had randomly picked out of a hat of twelve other southeastern cities. You can drive or fly or hitchhike or take the bus. The ambitious, I suppose, could bike or run, but this wasn't that kind of journey. I chose the train because, economically speaking, it was the most efficient choice. But really, I chose to ride the rail for selfish reasons. I didn't want to have to bother with goodbyes once I got to the port city of South Carolina. Surely whoever dropped me off would have hung over my shoulder for a while to make sure everything was OK.

And I'm glad I chose the train. Even if I had somehow known ahead of time that the ride would be uncomfortable and would arrive three hours late in Charleston, I still would have chosen the train. Riding out of Raleigh was well worth the first nerve-racking day of my quest. Navigating along Garner Road, the slow pace of southbound train number 5630 gave me an opportunity to say farewell to my previous life. Yep, that's the same Garner Road that takes you past the YMCA where I lifted weights with Bill, Charles, and Rod and where Jack had taught me how to shoot three-pointers with remarkable precision when I was just twelve years old. It goes past Rock Quarry Road, which takes you to Southeast Raleigh High School where Mr. Geraghty had inspired me to maintain my dreams on the basketball court but to also carry my education as a safety net, and past Aversboro Road, which will bring you to within fifty feet of the front doorstep of the home where I grew up. It goes past a collection of fast food joints and retail shops where I ate and shopped, but never worked, and past the sun-tanned tobacco fields that represent a lifestyle far beyond my comprehension, even for a boy from the south.

Past my past with a one-way ticket to my future.

There I was, alone in Charleston at the corner of Rivers and Durant, wondering if it would be wiser for me to go left or right or if pitching camp under the overpass for the night would be my best option. After all, it was getting late. At least I had assumed it was getting late. The actual time? Couldn't have told you. But it was well after dark, and I hadn't seen one person since I had walked away from the train station.

A big-body black Oldsmobile with tinted windows glided by with a suspiciously high regard for the speed limit.

The tattered map of Charleston that I had found on a vacant seat at the train station was going to prove to be useful. With it, I could more or less find my way on my own. Without it, I would be left to rely on the advice of strangers for guidance.

My first order of business was to find a comfortable place to sleep. Shoot, it didn't even have to be a *comfortable* place to sleep—just *a* place, a relatively safe place. As far as I could tell from the assortment of landmarks dispersed throughout the peninsula on the map, the action was happening south of my current location. Perhaps I was being naïve in what could have been a crucial mistake, but I figured that the excitement and opportunity of my new homeland were directly correlated. With excitement came opportunity, and I was looking for opportunity. Left it was.

After walking down Rivers Avenue, and walking some more down Rivers Avenue, the notion of time still hadn't hit me, especially with the expected 6:47 PM arrival time of the train prolonged. All I knew was it was dark out—pitch-black dark—and Murphy's Law had offset my mental preparations for the trip.

A guy asked if I had any spare change.

"No, sorry," I said. I thought about retaliating with, "Do you have some for me? Cuz, uh, I'm actually running a little short myself." But, of course, I didn't. I had always accepted and even appreciated the vagrants that strung a guitar or blew on a saxophone or showcased some other talent at the park or at a subway stop underground, but I had never had any respect for the laziness of beggars.

The sign under Johnson's Chiropractic Clinic illuminated 10:14 and 81 degrees. Wendy's and Captain D's Seafood appeared on the right, and my nerves began to ease. Finally! Something familiar. With a little more bounce in my step and determination in my mind, I made the executive—yet uneducated—decision to keep hiking toward downtown for my first night of sleep.

The nagging barks of dogs cooped up in distant neighborhoods didn't bother me as much as the cars whizzing by at blistering speeds. But then again, even the cars didn't bother me as much as the lightning. Terrific! Lightning. Murphy was on a roll.

Or was that just heat lightning? What is heat lightning anyway? Is that the lightning that strikes between clouds or between a cloud and the air? Is it going to rain?

What did any of that matter? Such thoughts were superfluous. It's lightning. If it rained, it rained.

The clock at the gas station at the corner of Rivers and McMillan read 10:30, and I was approached by a woman boozed up well beyond coherence. She counted out four quarters and ordered me across the street to fetch a bottle of King Cobra. I didn't realize until later that she had been banned from this particular convenience store and denied similar purchasing services from the locals. To everyone else she was "Diane the Drunk," the notorious target of ridicule and laughter. But not to me. Under normal circumstances, I wouldn't have thought twice about denying her request, but my current need to collect friends didn't allow me the luxury of passing moral judgment.

"You said you wanted a forty?" I asked.

"Yea, baby," she muttered. "A forty."

The gas station was filled with common people loading up on Smirnoff and Marlboros. From the agitated looks they shot my way, I could tell they were puzzled by the sight of a youngster purchasing a quart of cheap malt liquor late on a Tuesday night. Almost as puzzled as I was.

But never mind that. Diane was waiting on me, and more importantly, her King Cobra.

The $1.48 total came as a nuisance as I had to dip into the five-dollar bill of my original $25 to make up for the forty-eight cents that Diane had shorted me. If you had asked me three hours before how I planned on spending my initial $25, I would have handed you a list riddled with underwear, toiletries, bread, and, if completely nooooooary, a shirt or two. Dipping into my fund to pay the overage for forty ounces of malt liquor for Diane would not have found its way to that list.

Diane was waiting for me at the bus stop across the street, barking to the moon about how her boyfriend had left her for his homosexual lover. Six years ago. She didn't care that she owed me forty-eight cents, but she was grateful for my courtesy nonetheless. When I inquired about the location of the homeless shelter, she invited me to come home with her for the evening. As intriguing as her invitation sounded, "Naw, I'll try my luck on the streets," sounded even better. A bus ride was not in my budget, and Diane had no idea where the shelter was, so I left her in her stupor and continued down Rivers.

I walked across the street and asked a half-asleep police officer, whose patrol car was positioned in a speed trap, if he could direct me to the nearest shelter. He seemed bewildered that I was not concerned about the eight-mile walk to get there.

"Straight down Rivers, right on Reynolds, left on Meeting. The shelter will be on your right. You really should take the bus," he said.

Half expecting that he'd offer me a ride, my enthusiasm began to grow, but before my expectations got too big, a lady of the night approached the car and the officer addressed her by name. She told the officer that people were talking about me and that I should probably get going wherever it was I was going. Neither appeared interested in hearing my fabricated story about my deadbeat dad or my druggie mom or how I came to arrive in Charleston in the first place. Fair enough. I wasn't their problem, so I continued down Rivers.

Three people had asked me for money so far, as I'm sure they would have done with any newcomer to the neighborhood. One guy, Joe, spent five minutes telling me his life story (birth to present) before he asked, "So I guess what it all really means is ... Can I get a dollar so I can get something to eat?" He didn't appear happy with my refusal, and I imagine word was starting to spread that I was a financial miser. But I had no other option. A dollar here and a dollar there would exhaust my start-up capital real quick.

The streets became more obscure and my visibility became impaired the farther I walked. When I reached the Church's Chicken at the corner of Reynolds and Rivers, I made a very conscious decision that my trek on foot would have to end there. I couldn't see thirty feet to the right or left and groups were huddled together in front of me, so I wasn't going to continue walking that way. My current endeavor was serious, but it wasn't that serious. Conveniently, I stood in front of a bus stop anyway, so I decided that it would be wise to give in and take the ride downtown.

I took a seat on the cement bench that served as the waiting area for the bus.

"Hey man, how's it goin'?" a man standing by the stop asked with great enthusiasm. Assuming he was after the same thing as everyone else that had approached me, I replied, "Well. I'm doing well. Listen man, I'm sorry, but I don't have any money."

And then began his tirade.

"What the hell are you talkin' about muh' fucka'? I din't ask you fo' no money! I said, 'How's it goin'?' I din't mention a damn thing about no money! Why you stereotypin' and thinkin' I want money?"

"Whoa, man. Chill out." Our initial dialogue was so overwhelming that I thought he was kidding. "I promise you I'm not stereotyping. It's just that—"

"It's just that what muh' fucka'?" He cut me off. "It's just that what? You see me come up here and try to talk to you and you think I want money? Is that it?"

Some of his friends sitting across the street in front of the gas station were really excited about my appearance in their neighborhood. Country comes to town. They decided the time was right for them to chime in. "Get 'im, D! Get that muh' fucka'! He ain't got nuttin' on you!"

Their words were still echoing in my head as I weighed my options. I could unleash my fury and start pounding him, which appeared to me at the time, and even more so now, both unintelligent and unlikely. My story very well could have ended on page twelve.

Or, I could try to reason with him.

"Easy ... D. Listen, buddy." Realizing the seriousness of the situation, I was almost pleading. "I promise you I'm not stereotyping. Three guys have already asked me for money tonight, and I just wanted to let you know up front that I didn't have any."

He didn't seem to care. He began to circle me like a lion preparing to pounce on his prey. His face was fuming and his mouth was foaming. I stood up to take defense. He couldn't wait for me to say the wrong thing, but I wasn't going to.

"Check this out, D," I said, trying to reason with him and quick. "My pockets are a little light right now, but the next time I come up this way, I can assure you that my wallet will be fat and we'll go get something to eat."

My attempt at reasoning was simply fueling his fire.

"You don't get it. I don't want your friggin' money, you—"

As if I was being dealt my lone get-out-of-jail-free card, I spotted the bus coming down the street. It was the most assuring sight throughout the course of my experience in Charleston. Was I scared to fight D? No. Was I scared to fight D on that side of town? Damn right.

My impending battle with D ended just as swiftly as it had begun. The bus slowed to a stop in front of us as I was trying to prolong our encounter with small talk. Another thirty seconds and my night would have taken a very dramatic turn. I hopped on the bus as D hollered behind me, "Make sure you bring some money next time!"

I was the only person on the bus, which turned out to be the No. 10 route's last run for the evening and $1.25 well invested. The ride took fifteen minutes and the driver dropped me off right in front of the shelter.

Though dimly lit, the shelter was much more pleasant looking than the surrounding buildings. To the left of the shelter stood a convenience store barred shut to protect against late-night intruders, while a series of abandoned warehouses stretched to the right. The trash littered throughout the rest of the neighborhood was noticeably absent in and around the shelter's common area. Two large trees greeted guests to the shelter and they were surrounded by a yard abounding with bushes and monkey grass. I thought I might have spotted a weed creeping out of the mulch, but I was probably mistaken.

Welcoming me at the front door was a large white sign with red and black lettering designating my location: Crisis Ministries, 573 Meeting Street. I rang the doorbell.

No answer.

I rang again and waited. Still no answer.

I knocked gently on the door and steadily increased to a full-force pounding. A lady yelled from across the street that they were closed.

Closed? I couldn't even think of a witty response. How could the shelter close?

"They stop taking people at nine. You gotta show up at seven thirty if you wanna get in." For $10 I could stay the night at her place. Once again, an intriguing offer for inexpensive lodging that I quickly refused. On the streets, confrontations were in the open. Behind closed doors, anything could happen and nobody would know.

Shortly after I had begun to make myself comfortable on one of the two benches outside the shelter door, I spotted someone coming around the corner of the side of the building. Police officer number two for the evening slowly made his way toward me.

Sergeant Mendoza, his badge read, stood five and a half feet off the ground with an additional two inches whenever he boasted about his role in serving the guests of Crisis Ministries. I could tell immediately from his demeanor and the austere look on his face that he took his job very seriously. Clean-cut with the walk of someone on a mission—someone with important dealings to tend to—I couldn't tell if he was thirty-five or sixty, but his body was built like he was twenty. He had retired as an officer in the army and was presently the only officer in the Charleston police force who enjoyed the beat at the shelter.

"Excuse me, can I help you?" he asked, concerned.

"Well, uh, uh, yessir. I'm looking for a place to sleep."

"Well, uh, uh, do you think you would be more comfortable inside as opposed to sleeping on that four-foot wooden bench?" His wisecrack lightened the mood.

"Yessir, but I was beating on the door and the lady across the street told me the shelter was closed."

Sergeant Mendoza, who was addressed by everyone—his wife included—as "Sarge," went on to echo the same thing I had already been told. Residents are processed from 7:30 to 9:00 unless they have a late worker's pass. But they had room that evening for one more.

"You're on the wrong side of town to be sleeping outside," he explained. "You won't make it through the night out here."

He led me inside the shelter, into the place that I would call home for the next seventy days.

After double-checking with Harold, the front desk clerk, to make sure there was room enough for one more person, Sarge gave me the OK that we would find a place for me to sleep. If I had known about the sleeping arrangements at that moment, I would have known what a joke that was. There's always room for one more at Crisis Ministries.

After the initial registration process ("Fill this out," "Sign here," etc.) and a background check that returned no outstanding warrants, Sarge led me to a back room for part one of my orientation. What could have easily been a fifteen-minute crash course on *How to Survive in a Homeless Shelter* was stretched into an hour-and-a-half seminar that included an overview of the shelter, facts, statistics, a bathroom break, and even a one-man skit on how to let somebody cut me in line. "You might be called a sissy," I was informed, "but being a sissy is better than seeing a fight break out in here. Please, we don't need any more heroes in here." I was beginning to think that Sergeant Mendoza was extending our late-night session in an effort to relieve his own boredom, but I didn't care. I was mesmerized by my current situation, my entrance into a world saturated with dormancy, druggies, and deadbeat dads. A world loaded with potential but short on ambition. A world of independence—free from responsibility— where each day would be mine to seize, or, if I chose, to squander. High hopes for someone with only $23.27 left.

Sarge continued his spiel, detailing the three different types of people I would find in the shelter, the ABCs: the mentally afflicted, the bums, and the victims of circumstance. Without hearing my story (which I was more than prepared to relay to anyone who would listen), he assumed that I was an innocent victim of circumstance. He, like everybody else, didn't care to hear how I happened upon his front steps, but he explained that Crisis Ministries had the resources necessary to get me back on my feet.

He went on to discuss a variety of issues that were not to be disregarded carelessly by an outsider like myself.

Lesson 1: *Don't use the blankets from the floor; you'll get scabies.* I told him that my sleeping bag had a built-in inflatable pillow, but he was not impressed.

Lesson 2: *Keep your valuable belongings with you at all times. Things have a way of disappearing around here.* I had already planned on it.

Lesson 3: *Some of the guys might bother you or try to hit on you; ignore them and walk away.* All righty.

Lesson 4: *Don't go to work for the day-labor agencies; you'll get screwed. Go to the employment agency on Lockwood and get a real job.* Cool.

Before he took me on the tour of my new domain, he had to take a few minutes to respond to a resident who wasn't feeling well. I took his absence as an opportune moment to read through the *Men's Shelter Rules and Regulations*.

All guests must complete a TB Test with the nurse at the shelter (regardless of your last testing date) within five days of coming to the shelter. Failure to do so will result in eviction until the test is completed.

All guests are required to attend orientation with the Intake Coordinator and to work individually with a case manager in order to receive additional case management services.

Guests may not have alcohol or other drugs in their possession in the Shelter or on the Crisis Ministries' property.

Disrespecting and/or cursing the staff, volunteers, or other guests will not be tolerated. Fighting, stealing, or other violent behavior may result in immediate ban from the Shelter.

No smoking in the Shelter. Smoke breaks are at 9.00 PM and 10:30 PM.

All guests are required to shower on a daily basis.

Guests who choose not to spend the night at the Shelter will not be allowed to eat breakfast, to change clothes, or to be assigned to the Clean-Up Crew.

Chores will be assigned in the AM and PM by the Shelter staff. All guests are asked to participate in the clean up of the Shelter at some point. Failure to complete a chore will result in the appropriate consequence.

All guests' bags should be labeled. Crisis Ministries will not be responsible for lost or stolen items.

Chairs are the property of Crisis Ministries and are not to be removed from the building.

Crisis Ministries has a minimal number of lockers for rent for residents who reside on the premises regularly. All locker transactions are held between the hours of 5:00 AM and 7:00 AM **only**; *the morning assistant will assist you at the front desk. Locker rental fee is $1 per week.*

On the back was a list of the *Daily Schedule*.

Wake up is at 5:15 AM. All cots and mattresses must be picked up and put away by 5:45 AM on weekdays. Wake up is delayed an hour on weekends and holidays.

Breakfast is served at 6:00 AM on weekdays and 7:00 AM on weekends and holidays.

Everyone is expected to leave the building at 7:00 AM on weekdays and 8:00 AM on weekends and holidays unless a time change is deemed necessary by the staff.

Lunch is served in the Soup Kitchen from 11:30 AM until 12:30 PM. Monday through Saturday and 12:30 PM until 1:30 PM on Sunday. Shelter guests will be allowed in the Soup Kitchen for the first thirty minutes of lunch, and then the kitchen is open to the community.

The Clean-Up Crew checks in at 7:00 PM , and all other guests will enter at 7:30 PM, at which time dinner will be served. All drinks and food are to be confined to the dining area, and no food is to be stored in bags, lockers, or the dormitory.

Guests checking in after 9:00 PM must have a late worker's pass or permission from their case manager.

Guests may do their laundry at the discretion of the staff and their ability to monitor the laundry/cubby room.

Lights are turned off at 10:00 PM. Television is turned off at 11:30 PM.

When Sarge returned, he took me on the promised tour of the grounds. We started outside so we could "save the best for last." Behind the Men's Shelter, to the left of the shelter for women and children, he pointed out two crack houses that were running strong.

He showed me the line not to cross—out of bounds for all shelter residents.

"If I catch you on the other side of this line, you are evicted from the shelter for three days," he scolded. By the way that he spoke to me—respectful yet stern—something told me that Sergeant Mendoza didn't take much crap from many people.

He used his electronic passkey to gain reentry to the building through the back door, which took us through the Transitional Dormitory. It was very nice, elegant, almost. This was the suburb of the shelter, the "Hamptons" to the inner-city lifestyle of the shelter on the other side of the wall. Just as the name would suggest, it reminded me of life in my college dorm with an added European Youth Hostel feel. There were fourteen cubicles in one huge room, each cubicle complete with a bed, a chest of drawers, and plenty of storage space. There was a TV area with sofas and two computers sitting on top of black wooden desks lining the back wall. A mini-fridge stood next to the TV with a microwave on top. What struck me as particularly odd was how clean and tidy everything was. The floor was not dusty, the magazines on the coffee table were not flung all over the place, and it didn't smell anything like what I had anticipated. Sarge explained that through a graduated program I could work my way up to live in the Trans-Dorm, although I later learned that veterans of the military are given preferential treatment, so, regardless of my rank on the waiting list, my chances of being accepted to live in the Trans-Dorm were slim.

And then we walked through a back door and into the general population section of the shelter.

Disgusting. Reaching the immediate conclusion that daily showers were not enforced, my first inclination was to pull my shirt over my nose in order to extinguish the reeking stale body odor, but I didn't want to give off the impression that I was a softy before I even truly began my journey. Nevertheless, I was nauseated.

The expansive room was noticeably plain, with its white walls and white tile floors. No pictures; no decorations; no furnishings. The floor was lined with two rows of mattresses on each side of a four-foot divider wall that split the room in half. It was nearly 1:30 AM, so nobody was awake, although a few people rolled and moaned in their sleep. And the snoring. Oh, God, the snoring. There's nothing harmonious about the chorus of a room full of men snoring in unison. My college roommate snored like a warthog choking on his tonsils, so you could say I was used to it, but ninety-plus roommates added a different dimension.

Sarge walked me through the dining area, which was also jam-packed with sleepers. Now I knew why there was always room for one more at Crisis Ministries: if there's no room over here, then there's probably room over there.

We tiptoed through a back corridor, dodging more sleepers en route to the bathroom.

The repulsive appearance of the bathroom sparked initial thoughts of seeking alternate methods of maintaining my hygiene. My nostrils were still filled with the stench of the sleeping area, but it didn't block an entirely different odor from seeping in. There was no way I could use those facilities. A thin layer of grime lined the already green walls and the floor was spotted with patches of filth. Open stalls meant we were forced to endure the humiliation of relieving ourselves in front of our shelter mates. Two of the toilets, in fact, were covered in plastic (thus deemed unusable), and the other two didn't even have seats. *No seats? Where am I supposed to sit?*

The sinks were the cleanest part of the bathroom, although you couldn't see yourself very well in the splotchy mirrors, so it came as no surprise that the serious shavers brought their own mirrors.

The showers—four of them in one room—were an even more unpleasant extension of the bathroom. The mildew on the wall nearly changed the tint of its color, and the floor was overcast with spent Band-Aids and soap chips ground into the already grungy floor. I knew right away that I would be showering with my shoes on until

I could afford shower slippers, I concluded that the shower room hadn't been cleaned. Probably ever.

Yep, the inside appearance of the shelter didn't match the immaculate exterior that had greeted me two hours prior. The bathroom had been neglected for quite some time, and as disgusted as I was by the shelter as a whole, I had already come to terms with the fact that it would be my home until I could bank enough money to move out. And I was OK with that. After all, my alternative—sleeping outside and bathing who knows where—was far less appealing and certainly less secure. That was my home, and I was ready for it.

I lucked out when Sarge found me an empty mattress where I could sleep for the night. Before I went to bed, he looked at me and said, "You look hungry." He summoned me to the kitchen, where he tossed a few frozen chicken tenders in the microwave. He also scored me some potato salad and orange juice.

Freddy J, who had been living at the shelter for thirteen years—far longer than the one year maximum that the shelter permits—was having trouble sleeping, so he joined me at the table. Despite noticeable mental deficiencies, he was the nicest person I met during my tenure at Crisis Ministries. I inquired about life at the shelter, but he was more interested in talking about life on the outside, so we compromised and talked about the latest movies we'd seen. He only liked Kung Fu, and I liked everything except Kung Fu, so most of our midnight meal was consumed in silence.

Although brief, my encounter with Freddy J was my first with a fellow shelter resident. On his way out of the kitchen, he turned to me and smiled gently.

"Welcome to Crisis Ministries."

TWO

EASYLABOR

❦

"All right, Kevin Parker! Out! Get the hell out! You, sir. Out. Get the hell out."

It was almost 5:30 AM and this was Ann, the overnight front desk attendant at Crisis Ministries, making her third go-round of attempting to wake up the sleeping stragglers. Everybody got to hit the snooze button once, but if you weren't up after that, you were going hungry until lunchtime. And it was looking like Kevin Parker didn't have much of a shot at breakfast.

"I'm up, I'm up. Jesus Christ. Why does it have to be like this every morning?"

But it was too late. Ann was sending two others out the door with Kevin, and she was on the hunt for more. She wasn't one to mess around.

Most of the guys found it difficult to wake up before the sun every morning, while a few saw it as an advantage in occupying a vacant bathroom. Anxiety had rendered me sleepless for much of the night, and I could tell that it wasn't going to be easy to rise at 5:15 AM on a daily basis.

Nevertheless, I was up. My mattress was tossed on the stack, my sleeping bag was rolled up, and I had even managed to sneak in to rinse my face before they raised the kitchen gate to serve breakfast. A shower was not at the top of my list of priorities, since I wanted to be on the front lines to get a feel for how the breakfast system worked. And besides, a shower wouldn't do me much good without soap, a towel, or even a change of clothes.

The breakfast du jour was scrambled eggs, sausage links, grits, and toast. Royal treatment. *I can get used to this.* It didn't take long, though, before I was warned that that day's meal was an anomaly. "Most days we just get hardboiled eggs and cereal, but we got volunteers this morning," a guy in front of me said. I went back for thirds. And then fourths. Who knew when I would be eating again.

It was Wednesday, and I was scheduled to attend orientation at 8:30 AM along with three other men who had arrived the previous evening. Orientation was required for all new arrivals as a way to get everyone acquainted with the shelter, go over various requirements, and then assign a caseworker for us to meet with on a regular basis. Aside from determining who my caseworker would be, I couldn't imagine that there was much that Sergeant Mendoza hadn't already told me about the shelter.

As I was finishing the last bite of my morning meal, a guy walked in and shouted, "Who wants to work? Van's outside!"

Well, you didn't have to ask me twice. That's what I was there for. I asked Ann if it would be possible for me to skip out on orientation and postpone my TB test until the next day. I wanted to work. Impressed by my vigor, she sent me out the door with my promise that I would attend orientation the following day.

I hopped in the van marked "EasyLabor: Work Today, Pay Today," and we were off. I was almost certain that this was one of the labor agencies that Sarge had warned me against, but I didn't take the time to do any investigating. Even with unfavorable wages, "work today, pay today" sounded very appealing.

The driver swung us around onto Huger Street and down King. We arrived at a small white-brick building branded with the same sign as the side of the van. The twelve of us who had crammed in the van emptied out like clowns spilling out of a tiny car at a circus and into the building to see what type of work was being offered. The large front room was bordered with chairs and a table in the middle. A stale pot of coffee sat untouched on the table. As a new worker, I was required to fill out a form that struck me as less of an application than a data sheet petitioning my essential information—name, address, telephone number, social security number. I had two of the four. I inquired about the shelter information with another guy, but he said that none of that mattered. "Just write down whatever. They're not gonna contact you."

Blue-collar, temporary labor agencies, as I was going to find out over the course of the next week, are the pit of the employment industry. One might assume that they are out to create a mutually beneficial joining of their clientele—the employee to the employer and vice versa—but that was not my experience at all. For unskilled labor, EasyLabor receives a set price from a patron—generally around $10 an hour per worker—and they in turn send the patron as many workers as they need. These can be for any of a variety of second-rate jobs, ranging from construction cleanup to landscape maintenance and washing windows to more skilled labor involving framing houses and masonry. And the work is not limited to organizations that happen to be short on labor for the time being. Anybody can order workers from the labor agency if they need help with monotonous chores around the house or heavy lifting or whatever.

In return, we (the workers) get a raw deal. We don't receive anywhere close to $10 per hour. The average pay for unskilled jobs at EasyLabor is between $6 and $6.75 per hour, but after taxes and a one-dollar check processing fee and this fee and that fee, workers usually walk away with $4.50 tops. Forget benefits or any other perks.

The operation is advantageous to both the patron (they get rather inexpensive labor and they don't have to worry about insurance and other miscellaneous costs) and EasyLabor (they get a fat chunk of the action), but the worker—just as Sergeant Mendoza had suggested—gets screwed.

The kicker is that there's always a surplus of labor. Walk into any blue-collar labor agency in Charleston at around nine in the morning and you'll see an assembly of people who didn't get sent out for the day. The attraction of just showing up and working and getting cash at the end of the day is, to some people, superior to working a real job. True, some of the laborers are temporarily unemployed and some are working while they have days off from their permanent jobs, but still, others simply come to work a few days a week whenever they need cash. If they don't feel like working, there's no need to call the boss faking an ailment or yet another death in the family. They just don't go.

The lone clerk at the front desk, Angela, was announcing that she needed one more person to go to James Island to work for the waste disposal department. I happened to be near the desk, so I asked her how much the job was paying. Aggravated by the question, she looked through her paperwork and said, "Five ninety-five. You want to go or not?"

It hit me that nobody ever really asks how much a job is paying. Some workers are picky about going on certain jobs (one lady had told Angela, "I ain't doin' nuh-in' that got anythang to do wih' fish"), but few really care how much the job is paying. After all, the unskilled jobs through the agency all pay around the same.

"Do you think any better-paying jobs are gonna come up?" I asked, equally as persistent as I was annoying. She would have ignored me except that I was breathing down her neck. I was a gnat at her picnic.

"Maybe, maybe not. You can hang around if you want."

Since it was my first day and I didn't yet understand how the system worked, I decided it would be best for me to go ahead and be a garbage man for the day. How bad could it be? Sure, such mundane tasks like taking out my own trash had always proved challenging, but this would be better than doing nothing, and any money I could accrue on my first day would be significant for shopping for essential goods that night. Likewise, a day off would keep me a day away from attaining my goal.

"Nah, I'll take it," I told her, and off I went with two other guys who had been working on the same ticket for a week.

The EasyLabor van made three other stops before ours, and by 7:30 AM, I found myself standing in front of an unmarked metal building watching men in orange jumpsuits glide feverishly in and out, sipping on coffee as they stocked their garbage trucks with water coolers and other vital components.

The other two guys and I approached the supervisor, and I introduced myself. He was blunt. "I only need two people. I told Angela just to send me two people."

No elaboration. No apology. No, "But I'll see if I can send you somewhere else." To his credit, though, he could have sent me along as an extra worker (on the taxpayer's dime) just because I happened to be there, but he didn't. Somewhere along the line there had been a miscommunication, and I was the one that was going to suffer as a result.

The supervisor called back over to Angela who said she would send the van back over momentarily. I waited for the next thirty minutes by the bushes in front of the waste disposal warehouse. I was beginning to get antsy when a car pulled up and a younger woman who appeared to be in her twenties like me asked if I was Adam Shepard.

"We got another job to get to. And we're already late. Hop in."

Conveniently, EasyLabor was short one worker on a construction job that happened to also be on James Island. Cicely, my partner for the day, and I had trouble finding the place in the backwoods of a hidden residential community, but I didn't care. I was happy just to be working.

We arrived at a construction site where ten or so workers were already busy laying foundation on one building and putting up drywall on another. For a residential community, I couldn't believe the size of the buildings they were constructing. In later conversation with fellow workers, I learned that one was the main house and the other was the pool house, parts of an estate that were being built for a big-shot attorney from New England who had won a large settlement in a case with a tobacco company. Behind the layout sat a scenic inlet, which later turned out to be off limits for swimming during lunchtime.

"Big Bob"—whose name I learned from the tattoo etched on his right bicep—was the foreman of the project, and he didn't hesitate to greet us with a snarl. His white beard blew in the breeze, and his eyes squinted when he spoke to us. Intuition told me that he probably spent the holiday season at a shopping mall quizzing kids on their Christmas lists, but it was July and he wasn't playing Santa. "You're late. You friggin' people from EasyLabor are always late." We were supposed to be there at 7:30 AM and it was now almost 8:30.

He handed us off to one of his workers who showed us what we would be doing for the day: cleaning up the work area. The site was cluttered with discarded concrete forms from the foundation which had just been poured, and our job for the day was going to be to stack them to the side according to their size: short and skinny, long and skinny, short and wide. At first glance, it looked like enough work to last maybe two hours, contingent upon Cicely's work ethic, but I didn't have the fortitude to stretch it into a full day's work as it appeared some of the other guys were doing with their tasks. I watched one guy who was sitting on the rear stoop of the big house puffing on a cigarette, evidently quite delighted with his ability to get away with his masterminded one-two style: work one minute, rest two.

By 9:30, it didn't matter, however, since Big Bob showed his face sparingly to supervise. It was a typical southern summer day with the temperature in the nineties and the humidity making it seem even hotter. He had retreated to his F-150 pickup truck to hang out in the air conditioning, which made it easy for everyone to work at his or her own pace. And that wasn't at all a bad situation, since Big Bob was a very poor manager anyway. He would come out, bark orders, and then go back to the air-conditioned comforts of his truck. Nobody respected him. They would obey his instructions while he was around, but once he turned his back, they were right back to doing it their own way. Ironically enough, Big Bob had (by his own admission) earned the right to be lazy after years of his own hard work.

We finished stacking the concrete forms by 10:00 AM, at which point they had found plenty more work for us to do. We cleaned up miscellaneous trash, removed nails from boards, and filled empty holes with dirt. We broke for lunch at the neighborhood Piggly Wiggly, a southern grocery store chain, at 12:30 and Cicely and I split a lukewarm chicken dinner with green beans. I was already beat. The work was tedious, to be sure, but the heat was really starting to get to me. Cicely was in Superwoman mode, never stopping for a single break, and I surely wasn't going to be the one to interrupt that trend. The last thing I needed was Santa hollering at me. I fought fatigue and by 3:00 PM, we were done.

Big Bob gave us a full seven hours even though we had worked from 8:30 to 3:00 with a half-hour break for lunch in between. "Y'all can come back and work for me anytime you'd like." A full-time job, which he probably wasn't offering, sounded appealing at first, but the one arena I had planned to avoid on a permanent basis was construction. We thanked him and left.

On the way back to EasyLabor to collect the day's allowance, I asked Cicely why she chose to work so hard. After all, the biggest reason that we finished each task early was because of her remarkable efficiency. She had outworked me on pretty much every project, which didn't bruise my ego too much since she had been working throughout the summer with EasyLabor and she was used to the hot days working outside.

"The harder I work, the more praise I receive back at EasyLabor. And if they like you, you get put on better jobs and maybe even a permanent ticket."

I assumed that first day's ticket with McMaster's Construction was an exception to that rule, but I got her point: EasyLabor had a reputation to uphold and they did that by sending out their best workers to the best (often better-paying) jobs.

We arrived back at EasyLabor sooner than many of the other workers. My payment options were to receive a check (succumbing to the billion-dollar check cashing industry until I could set up a bank account) or, for a $1 fee, I could receive my payment in the form of cash via EasyLabor's ATM machine. I opted for the latter—a choice I hated to make, but I needed the cash right away to go to Family Dollar.

After taxes, a couple of minor fees, the $1 ATM fee, and the staggering $5 I had to pay for the trip to and from the job ($2.50 to the van and $2.50 to Cicely), I netted $28.61 on the day. My share of lunch had cost me $3, so now, with the $20.27 left over from my initial fund, I had $48.88 to spend on the necessary items I intended to buy. On our way out, Angela remarked that she had plenty of jobs for the following day, but I remembered that I had to attend orientation at the shelter, so I was going to miss out. Before heading to her home on the north side of town, Cicely dropped me off up the street from EasyLabor at Family Dollar, where I made my money count. All of it. I bought six pairs of underwear, a six-pack of socks, six white undershirts, a stick of deodorant, a toothbrush, toothpaste, an eight-pack of Ivory soap, shampoo and conditioner, a towel, a washcloth, a roll of toilet paper for emergencies, and a week-long supply of an assortment of potted meat and crackers that I would eat for lunch. Even though I had to skip working on Thursday in order to attend orientation at the shelter, and I was unaware of the weekend's work schedule at EasyLabor, I now had the resources to survive for a while.

Walking back to the shelter, I began to ponder a few things. After my initial meeting with Sarge, the only thing that I had disagreed with was his advising that I avoid befriending anyone. "You might think you know somebody, but you don't," I remembered him saying. Well, fair enough, but isn't that true in all walks of life? I knew before I even hopped on the train for Charleston that I was going to need a companion on my journey. Could I accomplish my mission solo, dodging in and out of people's lives virtually unnoticed? Sure. Did I want to? Nope. I knew that having somebody to hang with would not only make things easier, but it would also make my life more interesting outside of the confines of achieving what I had set out to achieve. Sharing the day's endeavors and goals and dreams with a friend was more appealing to me than tallying my bankroll after dinner.

I had arrived back at the shelter an hour and a half early for check-in, which was not enough time for me to get down to the library to e-mail my parents who were waiting to hear about my safe arrival. However, it left me plenty of time to try to get to know a few people.

Quite a crowd had already assembled in preparation for the 7:30 check-in. The spread was mixed. Loners sat by themselves off to the side, while established cliques stood around talking about news, the day's happenings, and the other established cliques. I figured the loudest talkers were the ones that ran the shelter life on the inside, so I resolved that it would be valuable for me to meet a few of them. Unfortunately, the loudest talkers were also the least accessible, and they looked at me—the new guy—as more of a nuisance than a prospective acquaintance. My problem was more than likely in the icebreaker, but I couldn't be sure. I just didn't know what to say. In my previous life, I had always been known to struggle when approaching cute girls, but I never suspected that I would have the same problem in courting homeless men.

Enter Omar Walten.

Omar—who, as it turned out, had been in and out of the shelter for two months now—was experiencing the exact opposite of my dilemma. He knew darn near everybody.

"Hey, Omar, what up, homie?"

"Hey, Omar, my man, how was work?"

"Hey, Omar, I saw Alyssa today. She was asking about you."

"Hey, Omar, your shoe's untied. Oh, gotcha! Ha, ha."

"Hey, Omar! Hey, Omar!"

He was the king of the shelter, a social chameleon who could talk to just about anybody from any background about pretty much anything. Although the camera flashes were absent, he walked through the shelter yard like a rock star on the red carpet. And he was a smooth talker, too, the type of guy that could sell a motorcycle to a wrinkled man in a wheelchair, proclaiming the entire time, "Listen here, Gramps. Wouldn't you rather be riding one of these hogs than that creaky old hunk o' junk?"

Omar was short and bald with a noticeably athletic physique, and he had an unkempt goatee. His entire persona, all the way down to the way he made eye contact, was very genuine. When he flashed that smile of his, his partner in conversation knew that it was time for him to smile too.

And he was coming over to me. He picked me out, I assume, because of our closeness in age. I was sitting on the sidewalk with my back leaning against the brick building, at this point quite removed from the crowd since I had yet to engage in any conversation worth continuing. I had somehow managed to meet the three guys in the yard that didn't want to talk (except to tell me to leave them the hell alone), so I decided it would be best for me to retreat to my own corner until dinner.

But there was Omar, *the* Omar, on his way over to meet me, the loneliest man in America.

"'Sup?" he asked, rhetorically.

"'Sup?" I replied. So far we had the makings for quite the primordial conversation.

"I'm Omar Walten. Who are you?"

"I'm Adam Shepard. I just got in town from Raleigh, North Carolina, and I don't really know anybody."

"Really?" he asked, glancing at the empty space around me, surely sympathizing that sitting alone on the stoop of a homeless shelter is perhaps as bad as it could possibly get. "You ain't kiddin'. What brings you to Charleston?"

I went on to tell my fabricated story on exactly how I had come to find myself in the city that some describe as the pride of the South. I had surpassed opportunities to go to college after high school in order to stay home and take care of my mom. She had acquired quite a taste for amphetamines and rehabilitation attempts had been unsuccessful. At the age of twenty-three, I had decided that it was time for me to either get busy making a life for myself or continue on the road to nowhere. My father, who had left my mom, my brother, and I when I was five, had remarried and was now living in Savannah, Georgia. We spoke on the phone on birthdays and holidays and we had seen each other just three times in the past eighteen years. As I saw it, now was an opportune moment to rekindle my relationship with him. I was excited to start school at the local community college, work, and enjoy a new life in Savannah.

"And then reality set in."

My fabricated father knew I was coming. He had all of my train information. In fact, he had even purchased my ticket, which was scheduled to arrive in Savannah the previous night just before 11:00. I had called him and left a message when I was in Wilson, North Carolina, to let him know that the train was running late. In Charleston, I called him again to update him on the schedule. And he was drunk.

I knew that my father had been struggling with alcohol, but I wasn't quite sure how that would affect our rapport. And I certainly didn't expect that it would affect us so soon.

On my phone call from the Charleston train station, he had essentially told me that he didn't want me to come. It wasn't a long conversation. In fact, it was quite plain. "Don't come. I don't want you here. I won't be there to pick you up, and if you come to my house, I won't let you in."

Wow. I didn't even know how to respond. I hung up the phone and found my way to the shelter. That simple.

It was a great story, one I had been concocting for two days, and as I was going to find throughout my stay at the shelter, absolutely imperative. Everybody had a story. In fact, mine wasn't even that impressive compared to many of the rest. It was our way of being accepted into the group. It gave us something to talk about, a way of relating to one another. It put us on the same playing field. *Hey, we all come from different backgrounds, most of which weren't normal. We're all messed up. Now, we can either get out or not.* It's also the reason why we rejoiced when someone got out of the shelter and into their own living quarters. One of *us* was getting out. It's always sweeter when you overcome adversity to achieve something than if you are handed your fate on that metaphorical silver platter.

In the long run, as I said, my fictitious story paled in comparison to many of the real-life stories that I would hear over the course of my stay at Crisis Ministries:

Leo had followed a girl to Charleston from Los Angeles. When he got here, he met her husband, gunfire was exchanged, and now he was at the shelter until he could earn enough money to get back to the west coast.

Rico, divorced and picking up the pieces from a life gone awry, had been struggling with a crack-cocaine addiction and admitted that the area around the shelter was not exactly prime territory for reform. He wanted to improve his lot so that he could be a better father to his eight-year-old son. Two weeks prior to my arrival, he had walked to Charleston from Georgetown, about fifty miles away.

Billy had hitchhiked to Charleston from his home just outside of Chicago. He didn't have any friends or family in Charleston. He was thirty-two and escaping his previous life, one that included a bitch of a wife, parents who didn't care, and a handful of dead-end jobs. The only thing that followed him to the shelter was a felony weapons charge. His intention was to work and save money and fly to Spain to live for the rest of his life. "Just as soon as I learn Spanish," he told me later.

"Easy E," who would become a good friend of mine throughout my stay at the shelter, also had a drug problem, which he managed to keep under control better than some of the other shelter residents. Easy wasn't a typical shelter resident, though. He had worked in Manhattan's financial district and made a lot of money, but he longed to escape the cold weather, so he came to Charleston with his brother to start a painting company. In the end, his brother had squandered all the profits to a gambling habit and now Easy was left to start over with nothing. He had an advantage, though. He was very talented, handy with any tool you put in front of him. He worked for EasyLabor, but he always went out on skilled tickets that paid at least $10 an hour. He didn't need to live at the shelter, but he didn't mind the conditions, and as he later told me, "The price is right on rent."

And the list went on. Robert, the leader of the clean-up crew; Carlton, who never failed to get on Ann's last nerve; "Can George" from Cuba who made enough money to support himself at the shelter by collecting cans from the trash; Smitty, a local man who went home to Summerville to see his family every weekend but didn't have a full-time job to support them for the rest of the week.

Wasn't my story their story? Wasn't their story my story? Weren't we all in the same situation, stronger because of our past and working our way up from nothing or, if we so chose, remaining stagnant?

Omar was fascinated by my story. He created his own ending when he told me how things would have worked if he had been in my position. "Shit, I'da taken my ass right down to Savannah and told my dad what the business was. He woulda let me stay, I can promise you that."

And he wasn't all talk. He was having problems of his own with his father in Charleston, but he wasn't taking crap like I apparently was. He lived with his father downtown on Spring Street, but he came to the shelter a few nights a week when he was too exhausted to deal with each night's impending confrontations. But, more often than not, he would merely walk into his father's house, they would argue, and then he would go to bed. It was not an ideal relationship by any means.

"It wasn't always like that, though," he explained. "I come from an ordinary, middle-class lifestyle, but my parents divorced when I was thirteen, and everything went downhill from there. Dad took off for Charleston; Mom remarried."

After high school, Omar worked a series of jobs that didn't show any promise for his future. At twenty-three, he came down to Charleston to live and work with his father, who soon developed an attitude problem, which was followed by an alcohol problem, which was followed by an addiction to crack-cocaine. Omar had been in Charleston for eight months, but he hadn't quite found a place to fit in.

"I hate it here," he said. "I mean, it's nice and all, good people, all this history and shit. Maybe it's my dad. I dunno. I just can't get in the right groove."

He didn't have the resources to get out, but even if he were to acquire the resources, he wasn't sure what would be waiting for him if he went back home to Michigan. He was struggling to ignite that fire in his belly that could potentially catapult him out of his current habitual way of living. He talked about school and getting an apartment and other ambitious pursuits, but the fact was that he had worked six different jobs since his arrival in Charleston, and he wasn't happy at his latest at a pizza parlor.

And I think that's why we hit it off from the beginning. We were both at the bottom and we had both come from similar backgrounds. Sure, mine was fabricated, but I played the part well, and besides, if we were going to work our way up together and enjoy each other's company in the process, our friendship would evolve into much more than our storied past. Forget where we came from; we were more concerned with where we were going.

The morning clean-up crew was permitted to enter a half-hour early—a benefit that only three people had played to their advantage. By 7:30 PM, the line stretched out the front gates. Omar and I were close to the front of the line, which was more important than one might think, since everybody who arrived before nine was admitted. First in, however, got mattresses; last in got to sleep with the roaches on the cold tile floor.

The check-in process was rather uneventful. We told the desk clerk our name, he or she gave us a meal ticket, and then we went inside to pick out a mattress and a plot of the room to occupy for the evening. Then it was on to the dinner line.

On paper, there were no assigned mattresses or even assigned spots to sleep, for that matter. But it turned out that it was going to be more difficult than I thought to find a post for my mattress since the choice locations were controlled by the shelter's regulars. Three times I was told to move and three times I dragged my mattress away amid a cloud of laughter.

Finally, I found a place to sleep in the front corner of the shelter nearest the fire exit. Nobody liked to sleep there because of its close proximity to the hustle and bustle of Meeting Street on the other side of the windows, so I was left to fend for myself in my own little nook. Even Omar avoided the opportunity to sleep near his new friend when he chose to set up camp in the dining room. I reasoned that dinner scraps fallen short of the mouths of my shelter brethren would be ideal bait for the unruly march of an army of insects that I preferred not to accommodate. But Omar didn't really seem to mind.

Dinner for my first night was spaghetti with meat sauce, bread sticks, and salad with Italian dressing. I learned to appreciate these simple dinners more than ham or meatloaf or chicken, since there was always an abounding supply. Meatloaf could run out quick, but more often than not I could keep going back for spaghetti until I was so full I had to roll to bed. We were human garbage disposals. The shelter rarely stored leftovers, but they didn't throw food away either. They served until the dishes were empty.

I was exhausted. I hadn't slept well the night before and coupled with the demanding construction work, I knew it wouldn't take long for me to pass out.

I rolled out my sleeping bag and placed my gym bag filled with my personal belongings next to my mattress. I remembered what Sarge had said about keeping our valuables with us at all times, so as I was going to bed, I tucked my prized possessions—my journal and my presently empty wallet—deep into my sleeping bag. I had less money than when I started, but as the lights went out, a smile of gratification crept over my face. I knew at that moment, more than any other time during my year in Charleston, that my wallet would fill up. I knew that I was going to succeed. Now more familiar with my surroundings, I knew what I had to do to make it happen. It wasn't going to be easy, but I had a plan, and now it was just a matter of putting my plan into effect. And I couldn't wait to start.

THREE

ANOTHER DAY, ANOTHER DOLLAR

❦

"**H**a! Y'all wanna play with *me*? Y'all mothers are crazy! This is like a sport to me! I love this! Ha! Everybody out! Everybody get the hell out!"

Ann was great. She didn't care about anything. Whether we liked her or hated her, she didn't care. Actually, she'd probably prefer that we grew to hate her so that we would get our acts together and get out of the shelter sooner as opposed to later.

But that didn't necessarily matter to us at that moment. Ann was kicking us out. Not just Kevin Parker. Not just one or two people. *Us*. Everybody.

Just like many mornings to come, nobody had taken the initiative to grab a mop and clean the floor. Everybody, including myself, knew it had to be done on a daily basis before we could eat breakfast. It was supposed to be like clockwork: wake up, gather our belongings, stack our mattresses, and clean the floor.

But it never went that way.

Ann had an advantage, though, an ace in the hole. She knew when she could kick us out and when she couldn't. If we had volunteers cooking a gourmet breakfast, she wasn't going to kick us out because the food would get wasted. If the menu was cereal and hardboiled eggs, she wouldn't hesitate to send us out the door.

And that's where it was looking like we were headed on this Thursday morning—not the way some of us wanted to start our day.

Where is that mop? I thought. *Give me the mop. I'll clean the friggin' floor.*

But it was clearly too late. As soon as Carlton was headed out the door, we knew it was time to go. He had pushed Ann's buttons so many times that he knew when to keep pushing them, just as he knew when it was time for us to accept our fate. Out the door we went.

My second day in Charleston had the makings to be a wash. Ann had forced us all out the door by 6:00, so I had two and a half hours of idle time to wait for orientation. I napped on the concrete outside the shelter, uncomfortable as it was, until the sun rose over the trees. Then I read the brochures I had picked up from inside the shelter on sexually transmitted diseases, drug abuse, and anxiety disorders. I also did my best to study the bus schedule, which I knew was going to be my main source of transportation for the ensuing months.

Twenty or so of the other guys meandered about the shelter grounds with no particular place to go. Unhurried, a few raked leaves or swept cigarette butts off of the brick walkways. I couldn't help but think that this is where it happened—this is where people disappeared, fell off the map. Younger runaways, still full of potential, were lost in the fray; thirty-somethings reaching the realization that things just hadn't gone as planned; older guys who had been my current age—full of such promise—when I was just a baby running around in diapers with Pablem on my breath. They were me once upon a time.

Contrary to what I had anticipated, Ms. Evelyn's orientation was not a waste of my time. I was bored at the beginning as she covered many of the same topics that Sergeant Mendoza had covered in his orientation: rules, how to cope with being homeless, how residing at Crisis Ministries was a privilege and not a right, and how most men who were starting over on their own stayed at the shelter for an average of four to six months, with a limit of one year. Then I perked up when she began to detail the wide variety of resources that Crisis Ministries had to offer.

It was incredible.

There was a legal team prepared to represent selected cases pro bono.

The nurse was in every day from nine in the morning until five in the evening to treat our aches and pains, and, more importantly, there was a team of doctors who came in every Wednesday night to examine people with chronic health issues. If we needed additional assistance, we would be recommended for further medical care.

Two psychiatrists were also on board to help guests who might be suffering from a mental illness.

Special programs for veterans were organized with the Ralph Johnson Veterans Administration Medical Center downtown, one of the premier VA hospitals in the country.

And most importantly, each guest would be assigned to a social worker that would help us to identify what exactly had gone wrong in our lives and what type of plan we needed in order to return to a self-sufficient lifestyle. We would set goals and meet with our caseworker on a regular basis—weekly or biweekly—to monitor our progress.

The system came as a shock to me. I had never expected that it would be so complex and ambitious. I could tell early on that Crisis Ministries was not like the shelters where I had volunteered in the past or the shelters that I had heard about. Crisis Ministries had an established regimen to aid its residents in getting out and on our own. They didn't judge us for our fall into homelessness, but at the same time, they hated to see us in that position.

Noticeably absent, though, from the laundry list of offerings at Crisis Ministries were programs involving education. Through our caseworkers, we could arrange to get our GED or enroll in the Associate's Degree program at Trident Tech, but what about those people that didn't understand the importance of such credentials? Wasn't a lack of education one reason that many people lagged behind in the first place? Shelters like the Helping Up Mission in Baltimore mandate that enrollees are working on some form of education, and they have one of the lowest return rates of all the shelters in the country, so wouldn't it be advantageous for Crisis Ministries to adopt a similar program?

After the group meeting, Ms. Evelyn met with each of us individually to discuss our situation and to assign us a caseworker. In my meeting with her, she gave me three pairs of socks, a water bottle, a towel, and a bar of soap. She also provided me with vouchers to get a state identification card free of charge, a discount bus card that I could use to ride the bus for fifty cents instead of $1.25, and a letter to give to the Department of Social Services, affirming my homelessness and allowing me to apply for programs such as food stamps. Then she handed me a coupon for the Goodwill store that I could exchange for two pairs of pants and two shirts.

I tried to tell her my story about my druggie mom and my alcoholic father, but she wasn't interested. "Save it for your caseworker," she told me as she signed a series of papers for me. It wasn't her job to lend a therapeutic ear, but rather to merely get me jump started in the right direction.

Ms. Evelyn keyed my essential information into the computer and then followed with a tutorial about meeting with my caseworker. Kazia, to whom I was assigned, was working on her master's degree in social work at the University of South Carolina in Columbia. She made the ninety-minute commute to downtown Charleston every Wednesday afternoon to meet with her assigned shelter residents. That was the only opportunity I would have to meet with her each week. If I missed that time and Kazia felt that I was not making a concerted effort to better my situation, I could be evicted from the shelter for a period of time that she deemed appropriate, usually three days.

After my meeting with Ms. Evelyn, I waited in the lobby for the nurse to call me for my TB Test. I had the opportunity to speak with a gentleman in a wheelchair who was new to the shelter. He was also new to the wheelchair. Two weeks prior, he had been run over, literally, by a drunk driver while crossing the street in North Charleston. He had bruises and scrapes and scars on his arms and face, and a series of teeth were missing from his upper gum line. He offered to show me his badly mangled legs, but I declined, preferring to just take his word. Of course the driver of the car had never stopped to make sure he was all right, so there was no telling who hit him.

He had arrived at the shelter on Monday. Without the ability to work and without health insurance, he didn't have the means to provide rent or food. So there he was at the shelter with hopes that he could receive the medical services he desperately needed, as well as legal assistance. It was just one more of the shelter's many tragic tales. One day, he was standing upright, walking independently with a self-sufficient lifestyle. The next, he was at the shelter, in a wheelchair, at the mercy of the staff at Crisis Ministries. Another innocent victim of circumstance.

"But I'm alive," he told me with a surprisingly enthusiastic smile. "Shit, a lot of 'em don't make it, so at least I got that goin' for me."

The nurse called my name.

In the treatment room, she explained more about why everyone was required to take a TB test. I learned that the sometimes-fatal airborne disease tuberculosis has become more and more of a serious health risk since the 1980s, especially in enclosed settings that promote its spread, such as prisons, hospitals, and homeless shelters. The disease is very difficult to cure, but Crisis Ministries manages to keep the problem under control by testing its guests before they have lived in the shelter for very long. The process began with an injection in the forearm. Within five days, we were required to come back to see if there were spots on our arm around the injection site. If there were no spots, then the results were negative and we would be allowed to stay at the shelter. If there were spots, though, then arrangements would be made for treatment, and we would be prohibited from residing at the shelter. The process was quite simple and took less than two minutes. I would have to come back on Monday so the nurse could inspect my forearm for spots.

After the poking and prodding was over with, it was almost lunchtime. A swarm of hungry shelterees and other people from the surrounding neighborhoods had assembled behind the building to be led into the men's shelter kitchen, which also doubled as the soup kitchen for the city of Charleston. The mid-day meal was open to everybody, and the long line that stretched around the building made me happy that there were separate lines for shelter residents and the rest of the community.

We still had to wait ten minutes until the doors opened for lunch. The topic of conversation surrounded the next day's "Free Ride Friday." One Friday each month during the summer, the Charleston Area Regional Transit Authority (CARTA) offered complimentary rides on all of its bus routes throughout the city. CARTA's generous gesture gave Charlestonians an opportunity to discover the efficiency of the bus system while hitching a free ride around town. And naturally, many of the shelter residents, me included, were excited about that. Well, all of us except one lady who didn't hesitate to protest, "Shit, it ain't even really worth it. That bitch be jam-packed with a gang of muthafuckas just ridin' around in circles all day tryin' to keep cool. Them buses be smellin' sum'm awful on 'Free Rod Fridee.'"

Lunch, it turned out, was the best meal of the day. It was always comprised of a combination of whatever the volunteers had worked hard to whip up in the kitchen and the food that Linda had accumulated in the Crisis Ministries truck from area restaurants. That first day's meal included chicken breasts, crab legs, meatballs, green beans, rice, salad, cornbread, and our choice of sweet tea, water, or soda. When I went back through the line for seconds, they had added pork chops and potato salad to the menu in lieu of the crab legs, which had disappeared rather quickly. For me, it was a bit unfortunate that lunch was the most varied meal of the day, since I was hoping to have a job as soon as possible that would prevent me from attending the soup kitchen.

And that's precisely where I was headed. The sooner I could find a stable job, the sooner I could get out of the shelter and into my own place. And I wasn't one to waste any time. At around 1:30, I was finished making runs through the lunch line and was ready for an afternoon siesta. Since that clearly wasn't an option, I elected to hunt for a job. I had my Goodwill voucher, but since I was out of money, I couldn't afford to get there. While my supply of white undershirts would last several days, I was going to have to live with my original pair of pants for another day or two.

I wasn't sure where to begin in my job search, so I began walking down Meeting Street toward the heart of downtown. I filled out applications at the neighborhood grocery store and KFC, but neither had a need for extra baggers or chicken fryers.

A longer walk down Meeting (past the Charleston Museum, the oldest museum in the United States) brought on an entirely different atmosphere crammed with chic hotels and elegant restaurants. A man at lunch had mentioned that Hyman's Seafood was always hiring cooks and dishwashers. "My boy Garcie works there, and he don't even got no legs," he had told me. I didn't have any cooking experience, but I could wash dishes with the best of them, so I filled out an application.

No interest.

Maybe Sticky Fingers was short on wait staff. "Uh, come back in about a month. Maybe we'll have something."

Moe's Southwest Grille? Nothing.

My faith was fading, but I remained fearless. I filled out applications at a few hotels. Forget the stereotypes that said that females were usually the ones doing the housecleaning. I didn't mind vacuuming floors and cleaning toilets.

Embassy Suites? Nada.

Charleston Place? "We just hired two new workers, but check back soon."

I even tried the famed Francis Marion Hotel at the corner of Calhoun and King, and they told me I didn't even need to bother filling out an application. They weren't hiring. "We got a waiting list," the front desk attendant explained. "And that list is long."

It was summer, the tourist season! Wasn't anybody hiring?

Just before 6:00 PM, I decided to postpone my job search until the weekend. It was Thursday, and I still hadn't contacted anyone to let them know I was safe. Penniless, e-mailing from the Charleston County Public Library was my only option for communication.

Hidden among the adjacent banks and federal buildings, the architecture of the main branch of the Charleston County Public Library shows downtown's blending of the old with the new. In contrast to other parts of historical downtown Charleston where many homes and other buildings have remained standing since before the Great Earthquake of 1886, the Main Library—built in 1998— matches a new era of construction also evident in the surrounding buildings.

But none of that was important to me at the time. I needed a computer. The librarian instructed me to fill out the Internet user agreement form before he led me upstairs to the reference section, which housed one of the library's two main computer areas.

And I recognized half of the people there! The library was filled with guys I had seen at the shelter who were spending their free time on the computers looking up sports scores or surfing the Internet for the latest news. One guy, Larry, was even searching for jobs online through the website Charleston.net. I was embarrassed. I had been trudging through downtown Charleston for hours, filling out applications, when what I really needed to be doing was searching online or, at the very least, making phone calls. *Welcome to the modern era, Shep.* Pounding the pavement was perhaps one way to go, but there was a far more efficient system out there that I could use to weed out the employers that were not interested in hiring me. (Looking back, I realize that I should have followed Sergeant Mendoza's initial advice and headed over to Lockwood Boulevard to the employment agency. There, at the government's One-Stop center, I could have filled out a profile on the computer for employers to view and searched the listings of a slew of vacant job positions.)

Larry showed me how to fill out a profile on Charleston.net, but my research time was cut short when it came time for us to make the half-hour trek up Meeting Street back to the shelter.

We arrived just in time for check-in. I arranged my mattress in my corner at the front of the shelter and got in line for a dinner of chicken, rice and gravy, and green beans—a common meal prepared by men from the shelter when we lacked the volunteers from area churches.

And then began a rather eventful Thursday night.

First, at dinner I became acquainted with a few of the fellas. Up to that point, pretty much everybody, except for Omar and Larry, looked at me as more of an annoyance than as someone they could accept as one of their own. I had always been awkward and out of place in social settings, and, for reasons unbeknown to me then and now, my goofiness was working even more against me at the shelter. It wasn't too much of a problem for me in my current endeavor, but I thought it would be rather boring to go through my entire journey as "the outcast."

So, I was sitting at one of the dinner tables, quietly munching on a dinner roll, playing the part of the geeky kid in third grade that never got bullied but didn't have any friends either. Everybody was leaving me alone. Omar wasn't there, so I was left to fend for myself.

Several of the guys somehow knew my name, which was convenient for them, because they were talking about Adam's apples.

"Hey, man," one of the guys said, thankfully interrupting my peaceful dinner. "You have an Adam's apple, don't you?"

"Um, yeah." From the sly looks being shot my way, I could tell that this conversation was somehow leading down the road to mockery, but I had no choice but to play along.

"And your name is Adam, isn't it?" he asked, giggling like a schoolgirl.

"Yeah."

"Well, how does that work? Do you still call it your Adam's apple?" His peers were joining in giggling.

I was a bit confused, but I retorted, with a deadpan, straight face. "Actually, no. I don't have to. I just refer to it as 'my apple.' And interestingly enough, my parents refer to it as 'your apple' when they're talking to me and 'his apple' when they have friends over for wine-and-cheese gatherings."

They loved it. As strange as our intercourse had been for me, they laughed hysterically as if it was the funniest thing they had ever heard. We joked about it for another two minutes. Adam's apples! We joked about Adam's apples!

And that was it. Just like that, I became accepted, part of the group. I began to learn people's names and where they came from and how they came to find themselves at the bottom of the social chain. I discovered aspects of Charleston that were general knowledge, and I discovered unique things about the town that one can only learn about on the streets. I heard stories of war, lost love, and crime that doesn't pay. I heard about times of triumph and trying times where $16-an-hour jobs disappeared to the production lines of Mexico and China almost overnight. They taught me where to sleep if I ever got kicked out of the shelter for three days for a rule violation and they told me where to go for the cleanest restrooms in town. One guy even showed me how to remove the cork from the inside of an empty wine bottle (inflate a plastic grocery bag inside an inverted bottle and pull it out quickly), an endeavor that had won him a host of bar bets in his previous life

They took me in under their collective wings that night during dinner. They were the teachers, and I was their apprentice. They talked and talked, and I listened. They didn't care about me, and I didn't care about me either! I was eating it all up. I learned more that night than I had during my last semester in college.

From that point, there was no refuting that I was in. They didn't judge me, just as I didn't judge them. You were either a part of the "in" group or not, either working your way out or being a passive member of society, preparing to grind it out for the rest of your life. I wanted "in."

Later that night I took my first shower since my arrival in South Carolina. For the first two days, my attitude had been, "Screw it. I'm not going out to the clubs and bars trying to pick up chicks, so why do I need to shower?" But then I really started to smell myself, and I decided that my personal hygiene did not deserve to suffer at the hands of my own disregard. There was no denying my pungent body odor and, just like one of the guys, Jerry, said to me later, "If you can smell you today, then somebody else already smelled you yesterday."

I wasn't sure how the shower system worked, so I took all of my belongings with me. In fact, I hadn't felt comfortable leaving my gym bag anywhere out of my sight, so I had kept it with me at all times. I removed my shoes only to take off my socks, but since I had already made the conscious decision that my bare feet shouldn't touch the grimy bathroom floor, I put my shoes back on.

While other guys would walk in the shower with a bar of soap and walk out and air dry or use a shirt to dry off, I came a little more prepared. From my shopping spree at Family Dollar the day before, I had soap, a washcloth, a towel, shampoo, and my counterpart in the shower room swore that I was probably one of the only guys in

Crisis Ministries' history to use conditioner. But what could I say? I like the way Garnier Fructis's active fruit concentrate penetrates my roots and fortifies my rebellious, frizzy hair, enhancing its natural curl and shine.

I took a long shower. I wasn't tired, so I wasn't in a hurry to get to bed, and there wasn't a line of people waiting to bathe since most of the guys that took showers had already done so earlier in the day.

Not that I wasn't brimming with confidence and enthusiasm before, but that clean feeling made me feel much better. I opened the packages of socks and underwear and shirts that I had bought, and, although I still had to put on the same pants I had been wearing since I left Raleigh, I felt rejuvenated.

I had planned on reading before I went to bed, but they turned the lights out early, so my only option was to watch TV. Since the TV only had two channels (and those didn't even come in very well), people brought DVDs to watch with Carlton's DVD player. Nobody really seemed to mind what the movie was, and although we usually had a wide selection from the assortment that people owned or checked out from the library, we didn't have much trouble agreeing on which one to watch.

That first night we watched *Crank* starring Jason Statham and Amy Smart. It was a new release—in theaters—and somewhere in between the sound fading in and out and one of the people *in* the theater *on* the screen getting up to go to the bathroom, I realized that I was watching my first bootlegged film ever. And it wouldn't be my last. One of the guys was scoring pirated copies of a wide variety of feature films from a guy around the corner for just $5, and we were reaping the benefits. One time he even took up a collection so that he could purchase a "package deal" of the illegal discs for our viewing pleasure.

Call me crazy, but those are the times I'll never forget. When I'm eighty and sitting in a wheelchair at a retirement home in Florida with little or no control of my bladder and the nurses are talking about how that old Mr. Shepard is "ringy as a pet coon," I'll be sitting back remembering those nights at the shelter. Those times when I was just hanging out with the fellas, sipping on warm soda, munching on stale cookies, and watching bootlegged movies. Down and out, back to the wall, can't get any worse. Not a nickel to our name, nowhere to go but up. Too cliché? That's what we were! Looking around the dark room, I couldn't help but admire the stark complexity of our situation. We sat on the bottom rung of all social and economic ladders, and we knew it. We knew we sucked. Yet there we were, gathered together in the dining room slash living room slash auxiliary sleeping quarters of Charleston's premier homeless shelter, our eyes transfixed on the TV screen, wondering whether or not the hit man Chev Chelios would stay alive long enough to settle the score with his nemesis. And on Friday, we could get up and either go to work or we could sit out in the yard, insignificant to the rest of the world, and wait until noon when it was time for the volunteers to serve us lunch. But eventually we would all get *it*; whether it was that Friday or ten Fridays from then, eventually we would all wake up and realize that we were tired of the meaningless monotony of our lives, and that it was time for us to get going on living. Either that, or our allowed year at the shelter would run out, and we would be dismissed to the streets. Then, we would get *it*.

Six thirty in the morning was the best part of my day, every day. No doubt about it. I was awake, I was clean, I was fed, and as the warm breeze hit my face when I walked out the front door of the shelter, I knew the day was mine. It was also reassuring to think that most of the rest of the people in the country were still sleeping or rolling out of bed while I was already out and about, getting a jump-start on the rest of my life.

Plus, it was Friday. Everybody loved Friday, even if it meant another day at the labor agency performing crappy jobs for people who didn't give a crap about us. And that's where I was headed.

Even in the early morning, it was an ambitious walk, safety-wise, but it was my only option if I wanted to work that day. The EasyLabor van didn't come to the shelter every day. Angela from EasyLabor had explained that Saturdays could be busy or slow, so I figured I'd work on Friday for a few bucks to go job hunting over the weekend.

EasyLabor had an abundance of construction tickets, so I went out on the first one that had a vacant spot. It happened to be located downtown on Cannon Street where they were turning a block of three-story houses into apartments, so I passed on the opportunity to ride the van and opted to take the two-mile walk. It was just after 7:00 and the ticket said to arrive at 8:00, so I knew I could make it there in time. That is, if I didn't get lost. Which, of course, I did. Well, I don't know if you would call it getting "lost" since I knew where I was, I knew where I was supposed to be, and I had passed by the construction site three times before another worker from EasyLabor came walking along and showed me exactly where to go. At least I had one more guy to be late with instead of arriving solo.

Ken, the foreman at the site, didn't seem to care that we were late. He handed us each a shovel and gloves and pointed to a pile of dirt. "That pile needs to be spread over there. Take your time, though," he said as he squinted up at the sun. "It's gonna be hot as balls out here today." Unlike other construction jobs, he apparently didn't have a budget to adhere to, so he didn't hang around to monitor our progress. In fact, I didn't see Ken again until 12:30 when I went searching for him to ask if we could take a lunch break. He was on the backside of the roof instructing the subcontractors on what needed to be done to build the window arch over the third floor.

"Sure, take a break," he said. "Take all the time you need. Just make sure that dirt pile is moved!"

Which it was. In fact, our work had been completed for over an hour. I had wanted to go find Ken after we finished, but my partner commanded me to relax for a while, and his body mass told me not to upset him. But then hunger pangs had begun to rumble in my stomach, and I couldn't wait any longer. I devoured two packs of peanut butter crackers and three cans of Vienna Sausage before I realized that I would need to ease up a bit in order to stretch my personal supply of food as long as possible. If my work ethic was going to be the superhuman power behind the success of my journey, it was looking like my appetite was going to be my kryptonite.

The EasyLabor crew on this particular job was five strong, three men and two women. The other three had been hauling cinder blocks from the first floor to the second floor all morning. Even though they had established an efficient system of getting the blocks upstairs, they still had nearly two hundred blocks left. I felt bad that they had been working hard while we hadn't really done anything meaningful, but that was a moot point. We spent the rest of the afternoon on those two hundred blocks. It was hot, damn hot, and humid, and the cooler of water that Ken had supplied had been empty since ten. We each took turns at the water hose in between trips up the narrow flight of stairs with a cinder block in each hand. None of us were afraid of hard work, but we also knew the effects that the sweltering heat could have on anyone that didn't remain hydrated.

Ken had disappeared to the hardware store by the time we finished, so we had to wait around for twenty minutes until he returned. While he was gone, I sparked a conversation with George, one of the neighbors who also happened to own the three buildings that we were working on. We discussed sports, Charleston, sports in Charleston (a short conversation), and Ken's impending bout of unemployment. Evidently there had been a budget for Ken to follow, and he had already surpassed it.

George invited us all back to the construction site on Sunday to do some work on the side, and I told him that I would be there bright and early.

"Easy, kid," he said. "It's Sunday. Go ahead and sleep in."

I explained to him that I was staying at the shelter on Meeting Street and that we weren't exactly afforded the indulgence of sleeping in, but that I could come whenever he wanted. With newfound interest on his part, we settled on 10:00 Sunday morning.

Ken finally returned to sign our ticket and with the $5 I saved by walking to work instead of riding the EasyLabor van, I netted $36.48, bringing my total savings to $36.48. I had already purchased all of the essential goods that I needed to survive for a few days, so I didn't need to stop by Family Dollar on my way back to the shelter.

I was off and running. I had money in my pocket and a smile on my face. I caught up with Omar just before check-in and we shared the day's stories. Things were getting tenser with his father at home, so it was looking like he was going to be spending more and more time at the shelter, which wasn't terribly bad news, since I felt we could make the ascent out of the shelter together. Even more on the upside, he had registered for classes for the coming semester at the local community college. Pending the results of his financial aid application, he would be enrolled in a two-year culinary arts program that would put him in a position where he could work his way up to be a chef at any restaurant in Charleston.

Dinner was lasagna—lots of it—and following a shower, I hit the sheets early after a long day of hard work. Angela had again mentioned that she had plenty of jobs for us for the next day, so I decided to delay my job search yet again. I was overcome with the anxiety of remaining unemployed, sure, but I refused to let those feelings get in the way of the task at hand. The cash that I could earn over the weekend would give me the freedom to enact a serious job search beginning Monday.

FOUR

BIG BABIES

❦

If there was one thing that I liked about working for the temp agency, it was the anticipation and excitement that came each day with each separate job. Sure, the pay sucked, terribly, but every day was a different experience. One day I could be a construction worker, and the next I could be a landscaper or a baby-clothes hanger.

Yep. That's right. A baby-clothes hanger.

A slew of department stores and retail shops at the newly constructed Regis Outlet Mall in North Charleston were putting the finishing touches on their floor layouts. My first weekend in Charleston happened to be the final weekend before the shopping center's grand opening, and several stores had received late shipments of their clothing lines, which was great for EasyLabor, as it had scored several contracts with Eddie Bauer, Nike, and an infant clothing store. And it was great for me. I was looking forward to a change in pace from the rigorous outdoor chores I had been performing.

When Angela called out the names (eighteen of us in all, most of whom were shelter residents themselves) of who would be going to each location, I began to realize, to my surprise, that our jobs were never selected based on gender. Six people were going to Eddie Bauer, eight to Nike, and the remaining four of us—all males—were assigned to the infant clothing store.

We piled into cars and the EasyLabor van and traveled twenty minutes to the mall. We were all dropped off in the same location in the back, and we dispersed to our specified locations. None of us had been on that particular ticket before, but we found the store with no problem.

And, of course, nobody was there to meet us. The store was empty, and the lights were off. No worries, though. It was 8:30 and the ticket said for us to start at nine.

But once nine o'clock rolled around, I was curious. At 9:30, I was anxious, and at ten, I was heated. The four of us had been sitting around on empty paint buckets or pacing back and forth for ninety minutes in front of the store while the workers for Eddie Bauer and Nike had been going at it for an hour.

Just after ten, and just before I was preparing to walk to the bus stop to head back downtown, the owner—an older lady drenched in makeup and perhaps 150 pounds overweight—came to open the doors. She had her arsenal of full-time employees with her, and she apologized for being late. Traffic, she said.

Traffic? On a Saturday morning in North Charleston. All of you? At the same time? Yeah, OK.

We were upset, the temp crew and I, but we also knew that we were defenseless, forced to succumb to the owner's beck and call. We were on her time. When she showed up, we did what she told us to do. When she was finished with us, she would discard us just as she would discard an empty canister of lipstick. It was a cruel system, and we felt victimized, but we took it. After all, our far less enchanting secondary option was to be without work for the day, and as I said, any work was better than no work.

Motivated by the understanding that I was working my way out of this destitute life, I remained back in the shadows and listened to orders. Our task, hanging the new baby clothes, was elementary and dull: cut the box open, remove a pile of clothes, place them on the correct rack according to size and color, remove the plastic wrapping, throw the plastic away, lather, rinse, repeat as directed. There was nothing exciting about our job that day. I just wanted to get through it.

On top of the monotony of hanging the clothes, we had to deal with the owner and her posse. While we were able to dodge the fussy ladies for parts of the day, it seemed that the owner had delegated the power to her cohorts to pick on the day labor crew at their leisure. And they took full advantage of that power. "Would you mind?" was replaced by, "Hey, that doesn't go there," and bathroom breaks were awarded with the understanding that we would "Hurry on back now." Occasionally they would even try to cheerily sneak in condescending orders with, "Hey, Anthony, how's it going over there, hun? Great ... Say, why don't we converse a little less and work a little more? I believe that goes on that rack over there. All righty? Super. Thanks."

As the one o'clock hour approached, they started to rush us. "We have to have these boxes emptied by the time lunch gets here!" Boy, if that didn't kick me into fifth gear. *Shoot, lunch? Now you're talking my language, babe. Hand me that box right there. Nope, that one. I'll tell you what. Let's get a little system going here. You open boxes and take out the clothes. I'll remove the plastic.*

Lunch? That's all she needed to say from the beginning!

A half hour later, we had completed an hour's worth of work. We emptied the last three boxes as the owner signed our ticket for four hours. It had taken some hard bargaining, but we managed to squeeze a little extra time out of her because she had arrived late.

"I've called the labor agency, and they're sending someone to pick you up," she told us. "You fellas can just wait outside."

I was pissed. I hated to work hard for that lady in the first place, but I had done it with the idea that we would be munching on pizza or sandwiches by 1:30 instead of the crackers and potted meat that I had packed in my bag. Nope. No lunch. Just a kick out the door.

Adding a little drama to the afternoon, the owner (Planet Plump, the guys had started calling her behind her back, in reference to her having her own gravitational pull) insisted on searching all four of our bags as we exited the store. To me, it wasn't a fair gesture since all of our bags had been stowed away in a corner while we worked. I saw it as one more opportunity for her to represent her control over us.

I didn't have a problem with her checking my bag. But Mario did. As we would later find out, he hadn't stolen anything, but he had had just about enough of the owner's absolute rule.

"Naw, forget that. You can go ahead and forget about checkin' my bag. You know good and well I ain't steal nuthin' from your stupid store. Ain't none of your clothes gonna fit me, anyway."

"April, call security. Tell them we have a shoplifter."

"Security? Are you serious? Yeah, a'ight. Hey, April, call security. And tell 'em to stop by the Nike store to pick up some running sneakers on their way over here, cuz I'm a fast mother."

With that he marched out the door—with us in tow. I had just met these guys, but I was learning that if there was one thing you couldn't touch, it was the chemistry of four poverty-stricken workers standing up against abusive higher power. We never confronted security, but even before he opened his bag later to show us, I knew that Mario hadn't stolen anything. He couldn't have. He had been working with me on the other side of the store all day.

Our concern for confronting security waned as we sat around back waiting for the van to come pick us up. And waiting. And waiting. Among many other lessons, I was discovering that few people in my current surroundings had any concern for time. Ann did when it came time to wake us up in the morning, and Harold did when it came time to check us in at night, but the bottom line was that my clock was set on the convenience of everybody else.

After we had waited for an hour, I garnered the nerve to go back in the baby clothing store to ask the owner what the situation was with our ride and if I could perhaps use the phone to call them again.

I couldn't tell if I was more upset by the fact that she said, "No, they should be on their way," or if it was the beautiful spread of meats, cheeses, and other sandwich toppings of which there was undoubtedly a surplus. Whatever it was, I lost it. It went a little something like this:

"Y'know what, lady? I'm sorry if this offends you at all, but you suck. And I mean that in the most mature way possible. I mean, here we are, four hardworking men at your service today, and you and the rest of these ladies do nothing but abuse us. You boss us around like we're just your little servants, here to do whatever you want. Sure, maybe that's what we are, but that doesn't give you the right to treat us the way you do. I don't know what it is with people like you—maybe you think you're better than the rest of us; maybe you're trying to vent your own insecurities. Who knows? That's none of my business. But what is my business is that we came and worked hard for you today and you treated us like shit. And that's just not right."

Even though I clearly did not pose a threat to anyone, I was surprised she even let me finish. By the end of my discourse, my tone had cooled from disrespectful to reasoning as in, *Don't you understand how you're acting?* But her state of mind did not fancy reasoning. She wanted me out.

"April, call security."

"April, there's no need. My point's been made. I'm leaving. But I'm taking some turkey with me. And this roll. And is that honey dijon must—"

"Out!" She was not amused.

In hindsight, I should have grabbed the whole platter and taken it outside to my new friends. I would have been a hero. They would have thrown me on their shoulders and paraded me around like Notre Dame did for Rudy.

I'm not quite sure where my newfound gall had come from.

I felt passionately about what I told her, but I never intended to approach her. Before I began my project, I convinced myself that it would be wise for me to maintain a low profile. I didn't want to draw unnecessary attention to myself, and I certainly didn't intend to intrude on a lifestyle that I was, in essence, borrowing.

But then I met the owner of that baby clothing store, and all of those inhibitions washed out the door as my pride sailed in. Just like many of my counterparts, I didn't care anymore. I had nothing to lose! I began to let myself be me. If I felt something, I said it. If I didn't have an opinion, I remained silent. I laughed if something was funny and didn't if it wasn't. It's who I was before I embarked on my project, and it's who I was gonna be throughout the course of my project and beyond. People could either accept it or not. I didn't care. Hell, what were they gonna do? Not like me? Fine! I'd rather have one friend that respected me for who I was than ten friendships built on faulty foundation. It's so much more fun that way, too. I didn't have to be fake or pretend to be somebody I wasn't. I didn't have to run around wondering what people thought about me and whether or not they liked me and this and that. Take me or leave me, folks.

With that said, I never meant to interfere in anyone's life—as I had done with the owner of the baby clothing store—but I suppose sooner or later you have to take a stand. Maybe my speech was vain and insignificant or maybe it clicked a button that encouraged her to change her way of being. I hoped for the latter, but either way, I had said my piece, and it sure made me feel better.

Outside, the other guys were still waiting on the van. I purposefully neglected to tell them about what I had done since I didn't want to give off the impression that I was trying to be a spokesman for the downtrodden. Besides, it probably wouldn't have aroused their interest anyway. They just wanted to get back to EasyLabor to get paid.

The EasyLabor van finally came after we'd been waiting for an hour and fifteen minutes. None of us said anything. We hopped in, went back to the office, and collected our money.

All $14 of it. That's right, $14. The $24 I had earned was whittled away by taxes and fees, plus the $5 transportation charge, which brought me down to $14. It was almost 4:00 and I had been out of the shelter since before 7:30, and $14 was all I had to show for it. I was infuriated, pissed, steam venting from my ears, but I didn't show it. Even with the adrenalin still pumping through my veins, I decided that one stand was enough for the day. Nevertheless, $14 made me question my notion that any work was better than no work.

Omar had been working for EasyLabor on a job around the corner, so I waited a half hour for him to get back to collect his loot, which ended up being three times my earnings. We walked down King Street to Marion Square, where college-aged kids were tossing Frisbees and footballs and laying out on the freshly cut green grass, soaking in the sun's rays. Older couples were walking their dogs. We admired the atmosphere right before us from which we were so far removed. We were homeless. Bums. We could sit and watch, but that's where the line was drawn. We couldn't afford to woo any of those women, and even if we decided to splurge our money, we certainly weren't afforded the flexibility to take them back to our place for a nightcap. Can you imagine that conversation? "Hey, fellas, this is my friend Jennifer. She's a student at the College of Charleston. Real sweet girl, majoring in, uh, Aeronautical Biochemistry or something exciting like that. A little too short and slim for my taste, but I'm not picky. I'll take what I can get for now. Anyway, um, she's gonna be sharing my mattress with me tonight." We were window shoppers. Look, but don't touch. Single and unfit to mingle. The few feet between them and us might as well have been miles. They were well out of our league.

But, if nothing else, that gave us hope and aspiration and something to look forward to. For some reason, there was something magical about sitting there by the fountain with a mere $50 between me and broke. Watching everybody else running and giggling and prospering,

SCRATCH BEGINNINGS

Omar and I knew that that was where we wanted to be. And we knew what we had to do.

"Roommates," Omar said. "We need to be roommates. That's how we're gonna get out of this lifestyle. We gotta do it together."

And I couldn't have agreed more. Together. We sketched a plan that would have us out of the shelter and into the projects in two months. "I know where we can get a place to stay for four hundred dollars a month," he said. "It ain't a pretty neighborhood, but it's better than the shelter."

I was a bit skeptical about residing in the ghettos of Charleston, but that was a mere technicality that we could work out later. Right now, we had a master plan on getting out.

We walked back up Meeting Street en route to the shelter. We picked up our pace as we walked through "Chicken Row," the assortment of Piggly Wiggly, KFC, and Church's Chicken where the delicious aroma of fried chicken wafting out of the buildings' front doors made it difficult not to dip into our pockets for a three-piece dinner with mashed potatoes, a buttermilk biscuit, and sweet tea for just $4.19. Whew, that was tough walking through there. But we couldn't spend our money. As much of a fiend as I was for fried chicken, a few dollars here and a few dollars there would hurt me. We had to save. Besides, dinner at the shelter was right around the corner.

But really, saving wasn't that difficult for me since there wasn't much I needed to spend my money on. I would have to keep myself clothed, and I would need to spring for bus fare when it came time for me to get around town to places that weren't within walking distance. Until I got a real job, I would survive on my staple lunch of crackers and sausage, but even when I was employed full-time, I would be careful with how I spent my money. While I absolutely believed in rewarding myself from time to time for the hard work that I was putting in, I had to remain within reason. I had to delay gratification.

— 60 —

And that was the name of the game. Delaying gratification. In my mind, I had to be prepared to put my wants aside indefinitely as I fought to attain basic needs. I didn't yet have the means to provide my own food, shelter, clothing, or an automobile. Nothing. So the more money I spent on booze or cigarettes or snacks or the latest pair of shoes that nobody else on the block had yet, the farther I would be from accomplishing what I had set out to accomplish. To me, money that wasn't saved or going toward other worthy means was money wasted.

Which didn't mean I was setting myself up to be a robot that worked hard all day and penny-pinched my entire paycheck. No, no. An occasional stop at KFC or trip to the movies wasn't going to break the bank as long as I understood that I was on a mission. I knew where I wanted to be, and I wanted to get there as soon as possible.

I loved the hours at the shelter. In and out early meant that I would stay focused on what I needed to be doing and that I would have a better shot at staying out of trouble and out of harm's way.

On the weekends, attendance was down at the shelter as a lot of the guys hit the social circuit, renting hotel rooms or staying with friends. But not me. Weekends meant I would have my choice of where to sleep, all the shower time I needed, and enough food to fill me up until Monday.

Before check-in, Larry searched me out to relay his elation that he had just scored a permanent job through Charleston.net. He wasn't terribly excited about being a garbage man, but he was excited about the guaranteed forty hours a week that came with having a job with the city.

"It doesn't matter what time we get done every day," he said. "We get forty hours per week no matter what."

He also outlined a laundry list of benefits that included health insurance and even a 401k savings plan. It looked to me like he was well on his way.

"Yeppers. I'm gettin' the hell outta here, bro," he said.

"Cool, man."

"Next week."

"What?" I asked, puzzled, startled almost, at how he would be able to afford such an ambitious move.

He detailed his plan.

"See, the place I want to rent is $650 a month. I bring home $1,100 a month. With the $400 I have saved up, I just need one paycheck, and I can move in. I already worked everything out. I'm gettin' the hell outta this place."

To a certain extent, I liked his attitude. He wanted out, and he had a plan, whereas a great number of people didn't and were freeloading at the shelter off of the generosity of donations and grants and government dollars that were attained through a rigorous and competitive application process. Larry wasn't a freeloader, but I was still a bit disappointed.

I *wasn't* disappointed that his math was off. He was somewhat savvy, but on his salary with a host of other expenses like electricity, food, transportation, and entertainment, it wasn't going to be easy for him to live in a place that cost $650.

I *was* disappointed, however, that he obviously hadn't paid attention during his orientation with Ms. Evelyn. She had explained quite clearly that many people land themselves in the shelter or end up returning to the shelter as a result of defective budgeting techniques. "Your rent should not exceed one-third of your monthly salary," she had said. Several times. Weren't poor financial decisions a major reason that a lot of people were ending up at the shelter in the first place?

Despite my reservations, Larry was set on moving out the next week. He wasn't interested in hearing what I had to say about finding a place that was cheaper and maybe even getting a roommate. He didn't even want to listen when I told him that the second bedroom he required to house the drum set he was going to buy was just not a feasible option. He had his mind made up, so I had to let the issue lay to rest.

Outside the shelter before check-in was always the most entertaining time of the night. At about 7:15 every night, Sergeant Mendoza, known outside the shelter walls by his full name, "Hidethatshit Sargeiscoming," would walk through the shelter yard searching for open containers of alcohol hidden behind benches and book bags. At least three times a week, he would catch a newcomer who had not been forewarned about the secret searches, and he would take him to jail, where he was processed and returned back to the shelter by nine, all the while cursing the Wrath of Sarge. It was routine, but it kept the shelter residents honest. As much as we could say that we hated his serious demeanor and ball-busting tactics, we all knew that Sarge was the lifeblood of the shelter. Some might try to say we were safe because the doors to the general population area of the shelter were locked on both sides, but the truth is that Sarge was our security. Few dared to step out of line, and he nailed them if they did.

The freedom to shower as long as I wanted on Saturday night gave me an opportunity to do laundry for the first time, a system that the ever-so prudent Easy E had introduced me to the night before. Instead of spending several dollars per load plus the cost of detergent, he showed me how I could use my regular bar of soap to clean my clothes in the shower and where I could hang them each night so that they would be dry by the time I woke up the next morning. Since I didn't plan on having more than a few changes of clothes anyway, it was the most sensible option. I could wash my clothes in the shower at night and by the next day they would be ready to wear again. Even though a washer and dryer could have done a more thorough job on stains, I saved many dollars using Easy E's system for a majority of my time in the shelter.

With evident ulterior motive, Larry invited me to sleep next to him in a spot left vacant by one of the guys who was spending the weekend away from the shelter. I declined his offer. I was in a funk, dissatisfied with my day. My first Saturday had left a bad taste in my mouth. True, my clothes were clean, and I was well fed, but I'd invested nearly my whole day to earn $14, and that felt like such a waste.

But I suppose sometimes you just have to toss those feelings to the side and look forward to the next day. And I was really looking forward to my first Sunday working downtown with George, the guy I had met at the construction site on Friday.

FIVE

SUNDAYS WITH GEORGE

❧

I was quickly catching on to the system at the shelter. Generally speaking, I wouldn't hear Ann's wakeup call until her second time through when some of the other guys were up and stacking their mattresses, but I would still have plenty of time to brush my teeth before I grabbed a mop to clean the floor. I was convinced that the reward of checking in a half hour early at night to shower before everyone else was well worth ten minutes of sloshing a mop from one end of the room to the other in the morning.

Sundays were everybody's favorite day. Several guys talked about Sunday starting on Wednesday. For some, it was the end of a long week of hard work, and a chance to finally catch up on a day of relaxation. For others, it was merely another day of relaxation. For just about everybody, though, it was Church Day. And Omelet Day. And Free Clothes Day. All rolled into one. Battalion Baptist Church would send a shuttle to the shelter beginning at eight o'clock every Sunday morning and ending whenever the shelter's front stoop was empty. Before the morning service, the homeless folk were served three-egg omelets loaded with bacon, sausage, tomatoes, peppers, and cheese and were given a bag of donated clothes to take with them back to the shelter. Every Sunday morning, shelter-ites would stand outside the shelter, waiting for the shuttle, giddy with anticipation, and on Sunday afternoon they would return from church with looks of satisfaction stretched across their faces (except Rico, who would walk out of the service every Sunday without fail, stomach full, clothes in hand, after all of the homeless people in attendance were, according to him, "Demeaningly asked to stand up and be recognized").

But church wasn't for me. Not that Sunday. My Bible was substituted for the rusty shovel and garbage bags that George handed me as soon as I arrived at his house downtown. And when he led me around back to the courtyard where his dog had been doing his business for the duration of the summer, I knew right away that I was going to be earning every penny of the $10 an hour that he said he was going to pay me.

You know the expression, "You better go to college or you'll be shoveling shit for the rest of your life?" It is a job that everyone aspires to avoid, a figure of speech that is never supposed to materialize into reality. But it does, and for me, it had. I chuckled sarcastically as if in amazement that it was really happening to me. There I was, alone, standing before nearly seventy mounds of dried, brittle dog dung in George's "Courtyard O' Shit," wondering if that was where dreams went to be defecated right along with Sparky's morning meal. I knew when I began my journey that life wasn't going to be easy, that I would have to be prepared to perform a wide variety of jobs in order to earn cash, but I had never forecasted that.

If you've ever shoveled shit, then you know, and if you've never shoveled shit, then you still know: as far as jobs go, it doesn't get much worse. There's no way to add glitz or glamour to it. Shoveling shit is shoveling shit. But as much as I really, really, *really* did not want to spend my Sunday picking up piles of poop, I never once thought about dropping the bag and leaving. Who would? Ten dollars an hour, cash! It was baffling to me that none of the other guys had showed up to claim their piece of the action. So I shoveled. And shoveled. Dodging one mound to pick up another, I realized that there was no secret to this job, no way to conceive a more efficient system that would get the job done quicker. I just had to drudge through it. Scoop and toss, scoop and toss. But, rather than feelings of discontent, each pile brought on the attitude that it didn't have to be that way. I didn't have to be performing those shitty jobs. Sure, for that moment—that Sunday and probably the next sixty Sundays—I would have to perform similar duties, but each week would bring me closer to where I wanted to be. School? My own business? Of course I had dreams. But while I wouldn't be going to school or starting a business on Monday, each loaded bag of crap symbolized a step in the right direction.

After I was done, George brought me a bottle of Pine Sol and a broom, and he showed me where the hose was so I could get the courtyard extra spic-and-span for Sparky. The entire project took just two hours, although it had felt like a full day's work.

I was ready to call it a day when George asked me if I'd like to pull some weeds. *Why not? What else am I gonna do with my life?* Keeping with my newfound tradition that nothing would come easy, George's weeds weren't normal. His weeds—pokeweed, mostly—had smuggled Miracle-Gro and other plant steroids into the neighborhood, so they looked more like overgrown plants that had been neglected for several seasons. It was a one-acre model—to scale—of the Amazon. That was the bad news. The good news was that he had enough work on that one plot of land adjacent to his own house, where he was planning to build a three-story apartment building, that I could pick weeds for the next five Sundays. The terrain was rocky (even more work for the coming months), so it wasn't like a Bobcat or some other gargantuan machine could come in and just tear it all up. These weeds needed to be picked with finesse.

I spent two hours on weeds—just as tedious as my previous task (although more sanitary). The sun was blazing straight on my back, so my work time was peppered with quick water breaks every fifteen minutes. This also gave me an opportunity to converse with George about Charleston's history and beauty and how some of its residents had come from long lines of Charlestonians, while others were former tourists that had visited and declared that Charleston was the place that they absolutely had to live. He would describe in colorful detail the places he'd been in the world—Italy and Spain were his favorites—and we discussed the drug epidemic in Charleston that was not at all limited to the lower classes uptown. He wanted to hear my story on why I was living at the shelter, but I deferred it until the following Sunday. That first Sunday had already been packed with plenty of stories. By two o'clock, I had put in an intense four hours of work, and I had learned a lot about my new town in the process. He paid me $40 and sent me "home" with a sandwich since I'd missed lunch at the shelter.

Smelly and dirty, I walked a mile to the other side of the downtown peninsula, through Marion Square, to the library. This would become tradition. For the next two months while I was living at the shelter, rarely would a day go by that I didn't pay a visit to the library. It would become my connection to the rest of the world. I recognized early on that everyone belongs at the library. For a moment, lower, middle, and upper classes all blend into the same intellectual melting pot. Whether surfing the Internet or perusing the bookshelves, everyone can find something to do at the library.

On that particular Sunday, Easy E had solicited the help of one of the librarians to find a collection of books on drug addiction. Through some course of philosophical realization, he had convinced himself that the best route for him to take in discharging his drug habit was just to quit. On the spot. I certainly wasn't one to protest, although I knew that Crisis Ministries had programs in place that seemed a heck of a lot more efficient than quitting cold turkey. But that wasn't my business. What was my business was that he had been invited to a mass baptism around the corner that was serving hamburgers and hot dogs. And best of all, he was encouraged to invite his friends.

Well, naturally, with a building full of homeless guys, word had spread quickly that the Baptist Church on the corner was serving hamburgers and hot dogs at their outdoor mass baptism. It was a common theme represented throughout the course of my time at the homeless shelter when churches ventured to increase attendance at their outings: cook food. They'll come for the hamburgers and stay for the service.

And they were absolutely right.

Of the two hundred or so people at the baptism, at least forty percent were, or had the appearance that they were, homeless, while the other sixty percent or so had shirts inviting me to follow them to heaven. Six of us from the shelter had arrived together and we spent a majority of the time in our own corner munching on meat fresh off the grill. A group of us were working on our third plate before we even realized that the baptism had already begun.

This wasn't just any baptism, though. Some big-shot professional baptizer was in town, so six churches had come together to invite members of the community—at their own inclination—to be baptized. The audience consisted of representatives from each of the six churches, there to lend their support, some singing, and a few "amens." A stage with a huge tub of water was set up in front of rows and rows of chairs. The setup reminded me of an outdoor concert. Those who had been convinced to be baptized, a majority coming from the streets or the shelter, lined up behind a curtain that was set up behind the stage, which completed the outdoor baptistery. They were then introduced by first and last name as if they were being announced among the starters at an All-Star game.

"Ladies and gentleman, it gives me great pleasure to present to you ... Miriam Andoluci!" the professional baptizer said. The crowd went wild and Miriam emerged from behind the curtain, timid at first, but then excited that the attention was all on her. She smiled and waved at the crowd as ushers directed her to the center of the stage where the miniature swimming pool was set up. This was *her* moment and nobody could take it from her. She stepped into the water, shivering with chills, as if she wasn't prepared for it even though the ten baptizees that had gone before her had reacted the same way. The crowd looked at each other and laughed, just as they had laughed along with the previous people that had set foot in the water. "Man, that must be some cold water!" A moment of silence was observed, and then the mass baptizer said a few words and dipped Miriam's body back into the frigid water. The crowd went wild, again, with "amens" and "hallelujahs" as they accepted yet another one of God's children. Someone—anyone—broke into hymn, and the rest of the crowd followed suit. Miriam continued to wave at the crowd as she was handed a towel and rushed off stage, the whole time smiling from ear to ear. People congratulated her and hugged her and told her how proud they were of her. For those couple of minutes, she was the Queen of Chucktown.

And then it was Rashid Carraway's turn. And then Craig Wilson. And then Kara Norville. And then Vicky Gondola. And then and then and then. They would herd them on stage and off stage like cattle, their newfound assembly of God's children.

But the generosity of the congregation did not relinquish once Vicky and Rashid and Kara were led off-stage. Those who had been pegged as homeless were given additional special treatment. One guy, Joseph, who had been living on the streets since his time had run out at the shelter, was given a bag full of clothes, food vouchers, and the invitation to come live in a vacant room at one of the churchgoer's houses. I couldn't believe it! There were these people—strangers, homeless people—armed with who knows what kind of background, and members of these churches were reaching out to offer assistance. Not just a few dollars here and there or a pair of pants, but a place to live! I couldn't believe it. You can call it God's will or whatever you want, but I saw it as the most noble act of selflessness I had ever witnessed.

But did the men I met take advantage of the services that were offered to them by the church? Did the baptisms and altruism of the church jump-start them in the right direction? As much as I would love to report, "Yes! They were saved by these saints sent from heaven!" most of the guys were back to their normal selves before we even left the parking lot of the church. They walked a block back over to their perch at Marion Square, cup in hand, asking for a dollar to get something to eat. Or drink. Or smoke. Just as I had seen many times in my life before, one simple act of kindness could never hold up against the lure of the vices of such a freelance lifestyle. They needed repetition to get out. While some were self-motivated and had merely stumbled through a tough time in their lives, most of them needed someone constantly in their ear telling them, "Hey, buddy! You in there? Cuz, uh, I don't know how exactly to tell you this, but, uh, you're screwin' up. Big time. But I tell ya what ... All is not lost! There's plenty of opportunity for you. Help is on the way, my friend. But check this out: I'm gonna need a little extra effort coming from your end."

And that's where Crisis Ministries came in. That's why the system at Crisis Ministries had proven, and would continue to prove, to be so effective. In the destitute world of homelessness, perhaps one act of kindness or one attempt to adjust someone's attitude could be dismissed or even forgotten, but that's not what Crisis Ministries was offering. They were offering help, day in and day out. There was no escaping it. Everybody, from the director of the center to the front desk staff to the families from the churches that served us food in the kitchen, everybody was there to help us get out.

At the heart of all the work at Crisis Ministries were the case managers. Every week they evaluated our progress, letting us know what we were doing right and wrong. They pointed us in the right direction for the services we needed—medical care, employment, counseling, childcare, and more. Every week. We set goals and followed up on those goals. Every week. It wasn't a situation where we met with them once and they moved on to the next guy. Every week. They were there for us until we were out. Even before my Wednesday meeting with Kazia, I had already heard so much about the value of the case management services. Easy E, a self-made man in his own right, had even told me that without his case manager, he might have fallen through the cracks already. And with his drug addiction, who knew where he might have ended up.

Surely, throughout the course of the baptism, any churchgoer that walked past me would have noticed the stench venting from my body after such a dirty day of work with George. They probably would have loved for me to assume the position on stage to get baptized just so I could rinse off in the pool, but artificial acts like those had always come back to get me in some form or fashion later on, so I decided against it.

By Sunday night—just my sixth night in the shelter—I had become part of the "in" group. I was checking in to the shelter a half hour early because of my participation on the morning clean-up crew, so I was able to pick out any spot to put my mattress. And nobody was giving me a hard time. I couldn't tell exactly how I had come to be accepted (or perhaps merely tolerated) within just a week of my time at the shelter, but I suppose it had a lot to do with the fact that I had come in and, essentially, kept my mouth shut. I let them come to me. If I would have come in and acted like I was somebody special—somebody superior to the life at the shelter, just as many before me had done and many after me would do—then my story perhaps would have turned in a different direction. People would be shunned and picked on if they came in and acted like they were above the shelter, like they didn't belong there. I had reached my decision to remain in the shadows mostly out of fear of the unknown arena in which I had inhabited, but by Sunday evening, I had realized that this indigent world was, if you were able to blend in, harmless. By Sunday evening, I had already developed an in-depth picture on how to get by in the homeless shelter. By Sunday evening, I was no longer "the outcast."

As the previous week had passed (from the train ride on Tuesday until dinnertime on Sunday night) I had been brainstorming ideas on how I could pick up extra cash—any extra cash. The airport was an hour away by bus, so I had thought about collecting luggage carts and returning them for the twenty-five-cent deposit as I had seen other guys doing in my past travels. It would have been a great plan at LAX or Dulles. But then I was told that the tiny Charleston airport services about seven flights a day to about two destinations throughout the Southeast, so returning twelve carts a day wouldn't even be worth making the trip uptown.

Going door-to-door cutting grass had worked wonders when I was ten years old, so I figured that soliciting the same service in Charleston could translate into easy money. I kept that idea in my back pocket as a last resort in the event that I was really hard up.

Then, at dinner on Sunday night, some of the guys started talking about donating plasma, which they had been doing for months. The process, as I was told, was simple and would yield an easy $30 if I could put up with a needle in my arm for an hour or so.

So, on Monday morning after breakfast, I decided to accompany Omar to SerumOn, where he donated plasma twice a week. Before I left the shelter, I showed the nurse that I didn't have the spots on my arm from the TB injection, and she signed me off as qualified to remain a resident. Then, using the voucher that Ms. Evelyn had given me, we were able to stop by to obtain my official state identification card. Conveniently, the South Carolina Department of Motor Vehicles was along the same long bus route that went to SerumOn, but even with their remarkable efficiency, it was 12:30 before we arrived at the front steps of SerumOn.

Situated west of the Ashley River ("West Ashley" for the locals) in an office complex with a host of other doctors and dentists offices, SerumOn sets itself apart with neon posters radiating out of the front window.

"Donate plasma here!"

"Save a life and get easy money at the same time!"

"Refer a friend and get $25!"

Despite the satisfaction that I would walk out with $30 in my pocket, the atmosphere at SerumOn had already made me feel sleazy. Even before I knew how the process worked, I felt like I was selling a part of myself. I was inviting the doctors and their assistants to have their way with my bodily fluids for a price. I was a plasma whore, but I was kind of looking forward to getting paid.

Eight people were scattered throughout the lobby, waiting for their number to be called to go make their donation. Omar already had his donor number, so he signed his name and went about waiting with the rest of the donors, but I had to go through the burdensome process of filling out forms and then getting a physical. A *full* physical, where they check your *entire* body for any health issues that could inhibit your ability to donate. But I played along. Besides, it had been quite some time since I had a full physical, so I saw it as getting a bonus check-up with a doctor to go along with my $30.

I was led back to the lobby where I waited for five minutes.

"Adam Shepard?" the attending nurse announced.

I stood up. "That's me."

"You're up."

Before they took me into the donating room, we detoured by a holding area where routine tests were performed with each of the donors before each visit. The doctor's assistant began by testing my blood pressure. Interestingly enough, my blood pressure was a little high, but I figured that could only work to my advantage in pumping the blood out of my system quicker than everybody else's normal blood pressure would. The assistant then checked my body weight and tested my blood for proper iodine levels. Finally, she asked me a series of twenty-five or so questions, determining my qualification to donate.

"Have you tested positive for AIDS or HIV?"

No.

"Were you born or have you lived in or received medical treatment in any of the following countries since 1977: Cameroon, Central African Republic, Chad, Congo, Equatorial Guinea, Gabon, Niger, or Nigeria?"

No.

"Have you injected illegal drugs with a needle in the last three years?"

No.

"Have you had surgery in the last twelve months?"

No.

"Have you had sex with another man, even once, since 1977?"

Man, '77 was a rough year, eh? No.

"In the past twelve months, have you had sexual contact with anyone that can answer 'yes' to any of the above questions?"

No and no.

"Where were you when Kennedy was shot?"

Huh?

"Just making sure you're paying attention."

I was in.

After proving worthy to donate, I was led to the donating room, an expansive area with stations lining every wall. While the process was certainly much more scientific than it appeared, for me the donor, it was actually quite simple. One of the three or four attendants on duty would finally get around to coming over to service my donation. He or she would stick a needle—a thick needle, not the type they use to inject the flu shot—into my forearm. Blood was drawn from my arm through sterile tubing into a centrifuge. The centrifuge would spin, separating the plasma from the cells and platelets of the blood. The plasma was then fed through another tube into a quart-sized plastic bottle, while the remaining blood components were fed through a second sterile tube that was connected to the needle and back into my body.

It would take four or five cycles to fill the bottle with the yellowish liquid. The length of time averaged around forty-five minutes and depended upon a variety of factors, including whether or not we were fully hydrated and whether or not our plasma was loaded with protein and iron. The more meat and water we had consumed, the more fit we were to donate.

The process was safe and secure. All of the materials—needles and tubes—used in the donation procedure were sterile and disposed after our donation. Our body would re-supply itself with plasma within twenty-four hours, and we could come back after forty-eight hours for another shot at $30. We were allowed two visits within a seven-day period, although some people would abuse that privilege by donating at the other plasma donation center in North Charleston in between their visits at SerumOn. By the end of tho week, they would have twice as much money as the rest of us, but I could only imagine that it took its toll on their bodies.

While we were in West Ashley, Omar and I had the opportunity to apply for several jobs—two restaurants and a grocery store. The opportunities were just as sparse as they had been downtown, if not worse, although the manager at O'Charley's restaurant told us to come back on Wednesday as he should have a couple of openings for dishwashers. We continued our search with the idea that we could always come back there.

Since Omar had the day off and I clearly didn't have any better plans, we made the trek up Rivers Avenue on the number-ten bus. Spike (who didn't have a single strand of hair on his head), one of the guys at the shelter, had told me to stop by the car wash at the top of Rivers Avenue.

"The turnover at car washes is ridiculous," he had told me. "They're always hiring. You just gotta show up."

And boy was he right. The manager, a gentleman with a Slavic name that I couldn't respell now or even pronounce at the time, offered us a job on the spot. No questions asked.

"Herde are your shirts," he announced in his heavy accent. "Be herde tomorrow at seven thirty."

I was a bit overwhelmed at first, with both the satisfaction that I was getting a job and with the idea that it seemed a little too easy. I retracted a bit and asked him what the pay was. He said that all his workers started at $6.50 an hour plus tips and received raises based on their performance.

"Sometimes you get quvick raise, sometimes you stay at six-fifty. You verk hard, you get raise."

Omar wasn't interested at all, although he tried to sneak out with the shirt. Even though I was in no position to be greedy with my salary, $6.50 was lower than I was looking for, so I deferred, making the determination that if I didn't have a permanent job by Friday, I would join the crew at the car wash.

That first Monday touring the Charleston area by bus was when I really began to discover that Omar was unique. We had plenty of time to talk, during which time I grew to really appreciate that he wasn't like the other guys that I would meet at the shelter, or, to be honest, like many people I had met in my life.

"I screwed up, man," he would tell me. He had this good job or that good job and one day he would just get fed up with his circumstance and either quit or cause himself to get fired. "I had a great job at Fresh Pickins. Nine dollars an hour. 'Bout to get ten. Then one day I just got into it with the owner, and I walked out. Worst mistake ever." He looked down. "They were 'bout to promote me up to assistant manager, and I'd only been there three months."

Omar took full responsibility for his actions. He knew that whatever cards he'd been dealt in his life (which had begun with promising potential, but had then gone downhill) it wasn't anybody else's responsibility but his. It wasn't his mom's or his dad's or anybody else that had helped him or turned their back on him. It was his, and he knew it.

"But I'm on course now, dog. I'm on course. We 'bout to get outta this bitch. We know what we gotta do." He was telling me things that I had learned over the course of my own twenty-four years, an attitude that I hadn't imagined I would confront during my year in Charleston, especially in the shelter. "It don't matter what happened yesterday, dog. Today matters. Even if we fucked up yesterday, today is a new day, and we can seize today. What do they say? *Carpe Diem* or some shit."

Monday was the first night at the shelter that I didn't get the opportunity to go back through the dinner line for seconds. The shelter was packed to "capacity," and after running out of the evening's first meal, they had to dip into the walk-in refrigerator to dig out more chicken to cook for the last fifteen or so guys who went through the line. Since I usually saved up my appetite throughout the day, I was disappointed that I was stuck eating only one plate. Man, how greedy was that? I was already getting a free meal and free accommodations, and there I was discontent with not getting seconds. But Omar never had that same problem. By way of barter in which he always came out on top with a roll traded for rice or the like, and inquiries of "Hey, dog, you gonna eat that?" he never left the table hungry.

For the first time, I went to bed without a concrete plan on what I would be doing the following day. While it wasn't an aggressive approach, it would give me the opportunity to wake up and go with the flow of the day. I had the freedom, financially, to ride the bus around all day long scouring for jobs, and now that favorable circumstances at O'Charley's and the car wash had relieved a lot of pressure in finding a job, I didn't have to go about my search with such anxiety. I would still go on an ambitious hunt, but I could carry the attitude that no matter what, I would be working a steady job by the following Monday. Although I was fortunate to be working with George on Sundays, hopefully my shit-shoveling days were behind me.

SIX

HUSTLE TIME

❧

"**H**ey, Adam. Don't you think it's 'bout time for some new pants?"

While he had tried to present his criticism of my attire in a half-joking manner, his point was well taken. My pants were getting to be repulsive. Ten minutes of scrubbing them down in the shower the night before hadn't removed the dirt stains that had accumulated, and the foul smell acquired from a week's worth of action seemed to be a permanent fixture. I knew they were in need of a good washing (in a real washing machine), but I didn't think it was that big of a deal. But then a homeless man remarks that it's time for a new pair of pants, and you get to thinking that it might be time for a new pair of pants. So before I even thought about where to spend my Tuesday—my one-week anniversary at the shelter—it was necessary for me to go to the Goodwill for some new threads.

There was no denying that the No. 10 bus was becoming my greatest ally. It picked us up right there in front of the shelter and then ran from downtown all the way up Rivers Avenue, right through the middle of Charleston. Anything we needed was along the way at some point: medical care, all types of shopping centers and malls, the county's community college, and even the Department of Social Services, where I would go two weeks later to get food stamps. And best of all, a No. 10 bus came every half hour, so we would never have to wait long at the stop.

I don't care who you are, the Goodwill is for you. Rich, poor, fat, skinny, ugly, pretty—everybody can find something at the Goodwill. Everybody. It's like a huge, year-round White Elephant exchange. Donate what you don't want, receive a slip for a tax refund, and then go in to buy something that you do want for only about $3. It seems like everything is $3 or less. Shirts—polo or button down? $3. Shorts? Pants? $3. Shoes? $3.50, but still. And most of it is name-brand stuff that has been passed on by people who have grown out of the style or the sizes. They even have furniture and lamps and weight sets and negligees and hardcover books for a buck, and the list goes on and on.

I was spoiled on my first trip to the Goodwill. Not only did I have my free voucher—good for two pairs of pants and two shirts—but I also happened upon the grand opening of a new Goodwill Outlet Store on Rivers, which was decked out with a wide selection of apparel from other area stores to go along with recent donations.

It didn't take me long to pick out my clothes. I even thought about splurging for a couple extra pairs of pants and shirts, but the timing didn't seem right. Who did I have to impress? As long as my pants could remain free from stains and odors, I didn't care if I got caught wearing the same outfit every other day. That's what all of my new friends were doing.

In any event, I knew that I would be returning to the Goodwill many times throughout my time in South Carolina and probably even after that. The money I would be saving at the Goodwill would mean more money to put toward a car or a place to live or furnishings. (Indeed, I would shop at the Goodwill for the duration of my time in Charleston and beyond. Five months later, I went out with a beautiful radio DJ in Charleston, and I looked good. Really good. *GQ* tendencies. Khaki slacks, button-down dress shirt, blue blazer, and loafers. I'm talking name brand stuff. Total cost of the entire outfit? $14.96. She stopped returning my calls—all of them—but I can assure you it had nothing to do with my dress.)

Perhaps out of laziness, but more out of my desire to save money, I rode the bus back down Rivers Avenue to the shelter for lunch at the soup kitchen. While filling up on greasy pork chops and gristly chicken legs, I had the opportunity to speak with a fellow named John, who ate at the soup kitchen every day but didn't reside at the shelter.

"They hirin' at Fast Company," he said, opening the conversation.

"Pardon?" *What? Pardon? Who says that?* Really, who? Words like "pardon" could diminish anyone's credibility in any social setting, let alone a homeless shelter.

"You the one tryin' to get a job, right?"

I nodded.

"Fast Company. It's a moving company up there by the airport. They hirin'. You can prolly get a job no problem."

Ah, moving. Why hadn't I thought about that before! I knew that challenging labor would be rewarded with higher pay, and I had never been one to shy away from a challenge. Shoveling shit excluded, how much more challenging could it get than hauling chairs and dressers and boxes around all day?

"They start you out at eight dollars an hour, but you can get a raise real quick if you know what you're doing. You know how to move furniture?" Every time he spoke, he had a mouthful of a medley of mashed potatoes and green beans stuffed in his mouth, so I would miss a word or two every now and then.

"Oh boy, do I," I retorted. My brother and I had completely destroyed my parents' furniture over five moves throughout the course of their divorce, but we had dragged dressers and rammed sofas through door frames, rather than taking the time to carry the pieces with care. "Wait. Why? You gotta have any experience to work for them?"

"Well, I'da thought so. But then my boy went down there and they hired him on the spot. He ain't have no experience. They just said here you go, and they gave him a shirt and sent him out on a crew."

Eight dollars an hour? No experience necessary? It's exactly what I was looking for!

"And the tips," he continued. "Some days them boys bring home more in tips than they make by the hour on the move. They move all them rich people and shit."

I asked him why he hadn't gone down there to check it out.

"What'r you, nuts? You think I'm gonna move furniture all day? Ha! Hell no! That shit'll tear your body up. I got me a good job down at the paper factory. Don't hardly gotta work at all. Just gotta put up with that God-awful smell."

By that time, we'd both nearly consumed our weight in pork chops and chicken legs, and I didn't feel like going anywhere that required walking. But I was too excited to sit around and let my food digest. This was the break I had been waiting for.

Southeastern summers are the worst. Hot and humid, sunup to sundown, every day. I had spent the day merely walking around doing a few errands, and I was sweating my teats off. I could only imagine what it was like for the people that had to work outdoors on that Tuesday. By early afternoon, it was 103 degrees. Not "feels like 103 degrees" or "Hmmm, must be sum'm like 103 degrees out here today." No, 103 degrees. Thermostat says 103. "Feels like" 130.

It was a good thing that I got an early afternoon start on my quest to locate Fast Company, because their office was hidden off the beaten path. Even if I had known where I was going, I couldn't have found it without difficulty. And since I wasn't familiar with any of Charleston, let alone the area around the airport, it took me two and a half hours by bus and foot to get there through bushes and over fences. I was in Vietnam, attempting to attack the enemy's headquarters all by myself. I was trying to find a shortcut, but it only prolonged my expedition. Exhausted when I arrived, I asked to speak to a manager.

"He'll be back in a bit," Amy, one of the receptionists, told me. "Is there something I can help you with?"

"I'm tryin' to get a job. As a mover."

She looked me up and down, surveying my slender frame, as if to say, "What exactly do you plan on moving? Lamps? What are you gonna do when you have to lift something heavy?" But she was polite, keeping her personal feelings to herself.

"Oh, well, you can fill out one of these applications, and Curtis will get back to you as soon as he can," she said.

Super. Another application. Just what I needed. The odyssey to find Fast Company had been far from an easy stroll uptown, and now I was left filling out yet another application. I always hoped to speak with the manager firsthand, but my options at Fast Company were limited.

I filled out the application. Critical information, work history, education history, military history, references. *Do they ever even look at these things? When it comes down to it, aren't our willingness to work and the fact that we walk upright simply matched with job vacancies?*

Curtis didn't arrive back at the office before I left. Amy tossed my application on a stack of what appeared to be sixty of the same application packets and announced that Curtis would call me as soon as he had the opportunity to look over my information. Ugh. Riiiiight. *'Kay, thanks. 'Preciate it. I'll just go home and wait by the phone. Tonight? You think he'll call tonight? Or should I stay home and keep the phone by my ear tomorrow, too?* I felt frustrated and unfulfilled. Another application. Another afternoon chalked up to the job search.

I did a little back street exploring and found a shortcut through the woods and along the train tracks, back to Rivers Avenue. At least if I did get the job at Fast Company, I would know a much easier way to get there in the mornings after catching the bus from the shelter. The five o'clock hour was approaching as I passed by the stop for the shelter and rode the bus on to the library to search the classified ads on the Internet and to check the profile I had set up at Charleston. net.

Nothing.

Nothing. Nothing. Nothing! No responses to the queries I had posted with prospective employers and no new postings for jobs. With low expectations, what I had anticipated to be an easy job search was proving to be much more complicated. I decided that the hour-and-a-half-or-longer one-way trek by bus to O'Charley's was not going to be worth the pay, and even the opportunity waiting for me at the car wash had left me wanting more. I knew that once I had a job, holding on and working my way up would be the easy part, but was $6.50 an hour as good as I was going to find?

The excitement continued at the shelter on Tuesday night. In fact, now that I think about it, the shelter was exciting every night. Between catching up on the day's happenings and watching as new guests tried to blend with the shelter veterans, every night brought a new experience and new drama. All it would take was somebody cutting in line or somebody inciting an argument on the wrong subject, and before we knew it, half of the shelter would be offering their opinions. And we loved excitement. We could be sparked by anything. If Jimmy somehow finagled his way through the line to get seconds before everybody else was served their first meal, you better believe that somebody would find out and then everybody would end up telling Jimmy what they really thought about him.

But most intriguing was the fact that it didn't matter what the subject was. If a guy stated, "Kittens are cute," sure enough, someone would support him just as someone else would interject with, "Kittens are a bunch of pussies." Dinner in particular would never be served without some argument or incident. But I suppose that confrontation was what kept us going, kept us free from the monotony and boredom of the everyday life of going to work and then coming to live at a stinking homeless shelter. Imagine that. Imagine waking up every morning at a homeless shelter, and then off to some dead-end job, only to have to look forward all day to returning that same evening to the same stinking homeless shelter with the same stinking men. Confrontation, interestingly enough, served as an outlet to keep us sane.

And the humor. Those guys were some of the funniest, most witty guys I'd ever met in my life. It was the most bizarre thing. One minute, two guys would be barking at each other about the last dinner roll or a bar of soap or the war in Iraq or whatever, and the next minute they would gang up on some other guy, making fun of the way he sounded when he snored or a word he had pronounced incorrectly. "*Ephipany*? Ha! Did that mother really just say *ephipany*? I got an ephipany for ya. You're a dumb ass."

Yeah, humor kept us going. I could pretty much count on getting a good laugh in every night. Larry never introduced himself to the new guys as a garbage man; he was "the chief sanitation engineer for truck number six of the James Island Department of Waste Disposal." Philly, notorious for always borrowing money, would walk up to an unsuspecting newcomer and say, "Hey, man, do I owe you a dollar?"

No.

"Oh, a'ight. Cool. Say, got a dollar I can borrow?"

We would all erupt in laughter at things that might not be funny to outsiders, but to us—deprived men refusing to be deprived of our dignity—it was hilarious.

One night stands out as distinctly comical. After dinner, Omar and I were playing gin rummy with a couple of other guys (and earning no respect; Spades was considered the only worthy card game at the shelter). A guy came by with a fresh new pair of denim jeans, relaxed boot fit. He was marketing them like they were the hot new thing and that any prospective buyer was catching the deal of the decade. "They're hot! They're hot! Get 'em now! Just three dollars!" Some people ignored him while others laughed at his attempt to be a nickel-and-dime hustler just like the rest of us. Five minutes (and two rummy losses) later, the same guy came through the common area. "They're hot! They're hot! Get 'em now! Just three dollars! Size thirty-eight."

Still no sale, although one guy inquired if he had any other sizes.

"What size do you wear?" he asked.

"Thirty-four."

"Well you're in luck! I'll be right back."

He came back a minute later with the same pair of jeans and a belt, a worthy attempt at selling them as one size fits all.

Still no takers, but he was persistent, convinced that he was offering the deal of a lifetime. A few minutes later he was back with one last round through the common area.

"Relaxed fit, boot cut! They're hot! Last chance! Just marked down! Two ninety-nine plus tax!"

He never sold the jeans, but I found that deals like that would come along nearly every night. Two weeks after my arrival at the shelter, I got a brand new pair of Adidas sneakers—crispy, still in the box—for $7. Tax included. They were a size or so too big, and they looked like snow shoes on my feet, but I learned that you can't be picky on the size when you're catching a deal like that.

Which reminds me of the cigarette trade. The cigarette trade was huge for me. Everybody smoked. People would line up for smoke breaks like they were getting tickets to a Sox-Yankees playoff game. It was the only time that we were allowed outside of the shelter walls after check-in. While I was one of the few non-smokers at the shelter, even my lack of desire to start didn't hinder my judgment that participating in the 9:00 and 10:30 smoke breaks was a key ingredient in my social agenda.

So I purchased a carton of Mavericks for $6 from "Cigarette Man." (Even though I never caught a few guys' names, some guys were only known by the product that they pushed. Throughout my two months in the shelter, there were always three or four guys—either in the shelter or waiting outside the shelter before check-in—selling products at a huge discount. We all knew—or could find out—where to go if we wanted DVDs or clothes or bulk cigarettes on the cheap.) With a pack of cigarettes in hand, I would always be able to answer yes when someone asked me if I had a cigarette. While the secondhand smoke was perhaps just as harmful to my lungs, I fought through it for five or so minutes at a time as I would have the opportunity to speak with my new friend. Aside from dinnertime conversation, smoke breaks with the fellas from the shelter were the most vital link to understanding where these guys had come from. It's where I really got to know Leo and Rico and Billy. It's where I heard about Larry's day on the garbage route and his struggles to get out of the shelter. It's where everybody talked about (nay, argued about) current events in the world of politics and beyond. Everybody had a story to tell, and over time, it became clearer that nobody minded talking.

But the cigarette trade wasn't just about my being taken advantage of on a nightly basis. Realizing that I would need to slow down with my generosity, I followed suit with everybody else in the shelter and started charging the guys to whom I had already given a cigarette. The going rate for a cigarette was 25¢. For whatever reason, everybody always had a quarter, but they rarely saved up to buy a full pack. So as time passed, when they came to me, they would either come to buy or trade. Two cigarettes could be traded for one 50¢ discount bus pass (good for a one-way ride on CARTA; they were given to us by our caseworkers based on need), or three cigarettes could be traded for a can of Coke. Early on, I became a hustler just like everybody else. While it didn't work quite as much to my advantage financially as I had expected, I got to know many people in the process. And it was so genuine! If there's one good thing about being homeless, it's the realness of the relationships. We were homeless! There's nothing we could offer each other financially, so we knew that whatever friendships we were able to muster came without ulterior motives. And I liked that. If the guy I was talking to knew that I was homeless, then he knew that I didn't have anything other than good spirits and good conversation to bring to the table. I could carry the conversation knowing that it wasn't going to end with, "Say, Adam, got a few bucks I can borrow?" I was one of them and they knew it.

The 10:30 smoke break on my first Tuesday night in Charleston also marked the first time in my life that I had ever seen any hardcore drug when I saw a guy holding two rocks of crack-cocaine in his hand. At first I didn't know what they were—they looked like over-sized bits of Chiclets gum—but then I saw him make a trade off with another guy, and I was able to draw my own conclusion. Instantly, I was taken aback, literally. My mouth agape and my eyebrows tightened, I took a step back. Frightened almost, I was filled with feelings difficult to put into words. I was remorseful and angry and, for some reason, guilty, all at the same time. I hadn't even touched the rocks, but I felt so ashamed that that had happened right there in front of me. Wow. Right there in front of me.

But that's how it works. I'd read plenty of articles and books and seen movies. It's one thing that drugs are everywhere in the media, but not until you see it firsthand or until someone you know is affected by a hardcore drug like crack that you really start to realize the reality of it all. *Wait a minute. Hold on a second. Was that ... ? Whoa, whoa, whoa. Holy shit. That was crack!* Even the stories I'd heard up to that point were taken with a grain of salt. Easy E's drug addiction was just that: an illegal, life-sacrificing drug addiction. I hadn't taken it seriously. "Those streets. Man, I tell ya, those streets are crazy. Hey, would you mind passing the ketchup?" I never took what I heard as serious as it really was. I'd read plenty about guys like him. Good life, faces adversity, turns to drugs as a means to vent his frustrations. But, for whatever reason, it wasn't until I actually saw those two crack rocks in that guy's hand that it hit home, that it began to really register with me as genuine.

And it didn't help my mental state from the witness of the transaction that crack is the worst drug of them all: highly addictive, inexpensive, and easy to manufacture. It's just too easy. For five bucks, crack will get you high as Ben Franklin's kite and wanting to go back for more a half hour later. You can't get enough. You have to have it. So you smoke it or inject it in your body for a week and then you find yourself hooked. And that's that. Not much you can do from that point. Prolonged use means severe personality disturbances, inability to sleep, appetite loss, and paranoid psychosis, all symptoms that I would see plenty of during my seventy days in the shelter. Crack ruins lives before people even realize they've been ruined.

Seeing those two crack rocks sitting so nonchalantly in that guy's hand, wishing that Sarge had poked his head outside by chance to witness the exchange, also brought home my preconceived notion that many of these guys had more than just a problem that a swift kick in the behind could cure. I knew going into my project in Charleston that alcohol and drugs and mental disorders ran rampant on the streets and in the homeless shelters of America, disorders that require rehabilitation and medicine and counselors. The only revolutionary discovery I was able to make for myself was that a lot of those guys with those problems didn't even seem to really want help. They were content with the release that drugs and alcohol gave them. A five-dollar high was worth much more than facing the difficult task of going through a rigorous rehab program. Forget the chemical imbalances that these drugs create in the user. In a completely sober state of mind, a lot of guys didn't even want to quit. While some looked forward to their weekly meetings with their case managers at Crisis Ministries, others ached at the idea of having to meet with them. And all they had to do was get high to erase their pain. Some wanted help, wanted out. Others had already clocked out.

On a smaller scale, don't a lot of us have those same problems? The guy smoking a Marlboro Red while chewing a stick of Nicorette gum. The adulteress going out with other men, justifying that it might help her become a better mate to her husband. The obese man that orders a Diet Coke to go along with his bacon double cheeseburger combo meal. What are we justifying, really? Do we even want help? Are we trying to kid ourselves into thinking we care, or do we know, subconsciously, that the fact is we really don't care?

One guy, "Hustle Man," who I truly grew to appreciate and respect during my tenure at the shelter, told me one day, "Adam, y'know, I love 'heron.' I love it. I know it's bad, and I know that it might get me killed one day, but I love it." He loved it! With a completely rational mind, he had no intention of quitting, ever. And that's not even the crazy part. He was the most ambitious guy I met during my whole journey! He would wake up in the middle of the night, every night, so that he could be out in North Charleston by 4:00 AM selling copies of *The Post and Courier* to cars passing by. He would be up at 3:30 on Saturdays and Sundays. He would buy a shopping cart full of the local newspapers for a quarter apiece from the printer and sell them for fifty cents. And the tips: "On weekdays, I walk away with an extra thirty or forty bucks a day in tips," he told me. "Weekends: sometimes close to a hundred." In tips! And he could make his own hours. "I sell when I want and leave when I want." He was well-grounded and business savvy. And he was consciously addicted to heroin.

As a side note, I saw Hustle Man several months after I had moved out of the shelter, selling those same newspapers on his same street corner. I bought a paper and asked him how everything was going. Hell, he looked good. And you know what? He'd kicked the habit. "I was injecting all of my profits into my body," he told me with a laugh. "A friend of mine bought a house two months ago. I was buying heron. I had to quit that shit." Just like that. Bing, bam, boom. One day he's got a needle in his hand, and the next day he's making a life-changing decision. Maybe his story was unique—going through a month-long bout of intense rehab to kick his habit—but then again, aren't all stories of overcoming adversity unique?

Every night I checked the tack board next to the front desk where Harold or Ann would post the phone messages they had received throughout the day. If an employer called, we were not allowed to take the call, but the front desk receptionist would take a message so that we could return the call later.

For the fifth night in a row, I had no messages. Nothing from Fast Company and nothing from any of the ten or so paper applications that I had spread throughout the Charleston area to go along with the profile I had set up online. Nothing. Nada. Interesting, right? On paper, my previous life had been erased, and there I was struggling along to find a job just like so many other people in Charleston and across America. Was I in over my head?

Maybe the job market was weak, or maybe I wasn't looking in the right place. Maybe we were in a recession. But whatever it was, it didn't matter. Ironically, the availability of jobs was irrelevant to me. I just needed to get one.

SEVEN

JOB HUNTING 101 WITH PROFESSOR PHIL COLEMAN

"**I**'m 'bout to get me a job. Shit. Y'all muthas can do whatever you want today, but I'm 'bout to get me a job."

Phil Coleman, one more of the resident nutcases at the shelter that nobody really paid much attention to, made his intentions known that Wednesday morning. He had his mind made up, and he wasn't going to accept anything less than coming home that evening with a job. He didn't even act like he cared what his job was. He just wanted one.

"That guy, Phil," the gentleman next to me said with a hushed tone. "He's had like fifty different jobs. He always has a different job. People say he can do anything—plumbing, painting, electrical work, masonry, frame houses. Everything 'cept keep a job."

"Okay, Phil," one guy said with a smirk. "You go get that job, buddy."

As easy as Phil made it sound, I had other plans. I decided that it would be a good idea for me to spend a couple of days punching the clock at EasyLabor so that I could pocket a few dollars while I continued to wait to hear from prospective employers. Even though it wasn't the job I was looking for, my fallback option at the car wash relieved both the pressure and anxiety that had come with the job hunt. If I had other job offers by the weekend, great. If not, I would make the most of my situation at the car wash.

Angela sent me out on a construction clean-up job downtown on Wednesday, a job that she knew would have me back at the shelter by five o'clock for my meeting with Kazia. It was a big day. After eight hours under the sun, I walked back up to EasyLabor to pick up the $38 I'd earned, and then I headed over to the shelter to meet with Kazia.

Kazia, just like everybody else, operated on her own schedule, at her own pace. My five o'clock appointment time simply meant that I had to be in the lobby ready to meet with her by then. She'd get to me when she could. Anticipating her running late and showing up at 5:15 was not a gamble worth taking. If, by some miraculous feat, she was running on schedule and I wasn't there to meet with her, the consequences could be serious.

So I waited until 5:25 or so when she was finished with her other "clients" and it was my turn to take the chair. She was earnest in the way she introduced herself—"Hi, I'm Kazia. I'll be your caseworker for the duration of your stay here at Crisis Ministries"—but she didn't need to tell me anything about herself. The shelter walls could speak, and they had already told me all about her. She was the best caseworker at the shelter.

Her office, which I suppose she shared with other interns throughout the course of the week, was well-lit by three lamps and an overhead light, and it was furnished with a desk, two chairs, and a couch. She was noticeably well organized, which probably wasn't too much of a task for her since she carried all of her notes and her computer with her wherever she went.

Whereas my future meetings would be mere check-ins to make sure everything was going well for me, my initial meeting with Kazia was more like a no-holds-barred therapy session. I told her all about my struggles, relaying my story on how I had come to find myself in such dire circumstances. She appeared a bit skeptical at times when it came to hearing about my druggie mom and my alcoholic father, only because I hesitated with my speech when she asked me questions that I was unprepared to answer.

"What kind of drugs was your mom addicted to?"

"Um, meth. Yeah. Methpham—Meth."

"Who's looking after her now?"

"My brother. Erik. He's my brother. He's looking after her now. He's, um, twenty-two. Just got out of the army. Marines. He just got out of the Marine Corps."

I wasn't very good at lying, but it wasn't her job to judge, rather to help me outline a plan to get out and on my own.

Unfortunately, the two people from the Career Services department at the shelter were out of town on business for the week, so I would not have the opportunity to meet with them until they got back, at which point I would hopefully be employed. But if I wasn't happy with my job at the car wash, I could always use the shelter services as a plan B. In the meantime, Kazia and I had plenty more to cover. We went through all types of budgeting techniques (which was easy for my time in the shelter since I didn't really have any regular expenses other than the bus and an occasional meal) as well as tactics that I would need to get back on my feet. My situation was a bit atypical of many of the others she was dealing with, since it was my first shot at independence. Up to that point, according to my story, I had never lived alone or outside the confines of my mom's reach, so Kazia and I spent extra time on basic concepts, like where to go for proper medical care in the event of an emergency. Medicaid was out of the question since I wasn't a single mother (single men rarely receive those benefits, I was told), but she gave me a step-by-step tutorial on what I would need to do to receive food stamps.

"We're here to help, Adam. I can promise you that," she said. "But the fact remains that if you don't take some initiative, you'll be stuck in here like a lot of these other guys." Her speech was energized and her tone appeared unrehearsed as if she said what she meant and meant what she said.

While she was only six months or so into her employment at the shelter, she had heard countless stories of repeat visitors to the shelter, guys who did what it took to get out for a month or more but didn't have the preparation needed to stay out. It was a vicious cycle that had claimed many victims, and it was the only frustrating part of her job. Otherwise, she appeared to love what she was doing. While her friends were doubtlessly accepting high-paying jobs as accountants and managers and attorneys, she was doing something more worthwhile. She was making a difference.

She shuffled me out the door as she called in her next appointment. It was only six o'clock, so I had time to make it down to the library for a quick half-hour session on the computer, just enough time to check up on current events and to confirm my continued lack of interest from the local job market.

I hadn't seen Omar the night before, but I caught up with him when I got back to the shelter. He appeared disheartened.

"What's up with you?" I asked.

He smacked his lips. "Man, I ain't goin' to school. They ain't givin' me any money."

Since he didn't file a tax return, his financial aid hadn't gone through in time, so he couldn't register for classes until the next semester. He wasn't as angry or agitated as he was dispirited.

"It's ridiculous, dog," he told me. "I'm finally tryin' to do the right thing—go to school, work hard, all that. I'm finally tryin' to get my life on track, Shep. What the fuck?"

I really thought he was going to start crying.

But there was no time for that. *Suck it up, buddy. Just like the rest of us.* He would just work for the rest of the year, until it was time for him to start school in January. He started talking a bunch of gibberish about how he might move back up to Michigan to live with his mom and start his life over—again—something he didn't want to do, but things simply weren't working out for him like he had planned in Charleston. He was growing to like his new town if he could only find some source of inspiration to get him motivated. He wasn't any more pepped up when I told him that I was planning to start at the car wash on Monday. "Dude, six fifty an hour? That's like slave labor. You can find something better than that."

At dinner Wednesday night, I met a man named James who had fought through a bitter divorce eight years prior, in which his wife got nearly all of his assets—house, furniture, car. Everything.

"I was hurtin', man," he said. "Hurtin' real bad. I was stayin' with my ma."

Forty-two years old and living with his mom for support, he took some time to save enough money to get out and on his own. Revived and poised to conquer the world, he got his own place.

"And then my ex came back to me. Said she was struggling herself, that she loved me and that she wanted to give it another chance. So I did."

He and his wife got back together and began to build a life again. Things were going great. Then, another divorce.

"I'm *not* the only guy I know that has lost his hat, ass, and overcoat in a divorce. I *am* the only guy I know that has lost his hat, ass, and overcoat to the same woman. Twice."

Nearing fifty, his pride was one of the many things he lost in the second divorce. So, he came to Crisis Ministries to get back on his feet.

The services provided by Crisis Ministries, though, weren't what helped James get his swagger back. It wasn't even his case manager. It was a fellow resident at the shelter.

"This guy had been staying at the shelter for almost a year, and his time at the shelter was running out. One day he pulled out his wallet and showed me an assload of money. I'm talkin' 'bout thousands of dollars in cash."

The guy had been saving up all of his money for almost a year. He had a steady job, family, and friends, but he wanted to make sure that he never had to resort to that lifestyle again. He wanted out and he wanted to stay out. His lack of expenses at the shelter enabled him to save up to pay for the down payment on a duplex in North Charleston, in which he would live in one side and rent out the other. Putting up with the shelter for a year had put that man in a position that he would never be one or two paychecks away from living at the shelter. He had security. He was prepared to confront financial disaster.

While James had no intention of staying at the shelter for a full year, it was that man's attitude that fueled a completely different approach to living.

"I always had to have a fancy car with chrome rims and nice clothes. If you can afford it, cool. But if you can't, you don't need that shit. Right now, I just want my own restaurant."

He had brought up a good point about society in America as a whole, not just the homeless shelter. Are we very economically savvy? A lot of us spend our lives living beyond our means, working for items that aren't necessarily within our reach. We rack up credit card debt and spend money on material items and vacations that we can't quite afford. We splurge for a private-school education for our children, but then we offset it when we buy them the latest, mind-numbing video-game system and all of the cool games to go along with it. And we live in luxury homes and condos that we can't even enjoy, because we have to work overtime to cover the mortgage payment. Why? Because we don't know any better? Or are we compensating for a life that we didn't have growing up? Couldn't we be putting our money toward more worthwhile pursuits, like James intended to do with his own restaurant?

There was one more story that James told me that night. He had met a lady while he was living in Jacksonville several years before. She was homeless and in desperate financial need. Social services had taken her children and she needed to prove that she could support them before they would hand the children back over to her.

So she sat on the street corner. But, rather than sitting there with a cup in hand, begging for spare change, she held up a sign: IF I HAD A MOWER AND A TRUCK, I COULD START CUTTING GRASS AND MAYBE EVEN CREATE A FEW JOBS.

James rode by the same street corner every day, and for a month straight, he saw her sitting out there with her sign. Wind, rain, humidity, whatever. Didn't matter. She was out there, every day, for a month.

And then one day, *Poof!* She was gone. He never saw her again.

"I can't say for certain what happened to her. I'd like to think that she got her mower and her truck, and that she is doing well, but there's no tellin'." But that wasn't the point. It was her attitude that inspired James. She wanted out, and she knew what to do.

I spoke with James for nearly an hour that Wednesday night, and it helped me to gain insight into yet another homeless man's life. He was different from many of the other guys. In fact, he shunned them, telling me that they never listened when he told them the same stories that he was telling me. I thought he was right on target with what he had to say (although a complete idiot for going back to his ex-wife).

"Some of these guys want out, but most of them don't," he told me with an escalated tone, hoping that somebody would hear him and try to prove him wrong. "They'll be journeymen for the rest of their lives."

Sarge came through the common area, calling out some guy's name that he needed to speak to. Nobody came forward. I often wondered who Sarge was looking for when he came through calling out names. He had busted two guys from "America's Most Wanted" in his nearly ten years on duty at the shelter, so I'm sure he was always looking for his next big bust.

Which also really got me wondering about Sarge's motive. What kept that man coming back to the shelter five nights a week for a beat that the other officers shied away from or took lightly? Even when the shelter residents would poke fun at him for the way that he took his job so seriously, disciplining even the most minor offenses, what inspired him to stay true to his own personal code of ethics?

When I asked him what motivated him, he simply told me, heroically, "I go where I'm needed, and they need me here," but I know it was more than that. He had been there for almost a decade, ever since his retirement from the army, and it was evident that he loved serving and protecting the residents at the shelter. You could see it in the way he prowled around the shelter, eyes squinted, like he was preparing for a night ambush. Working at the shelter filled him with a sense of nobility, like his chosen occupation wasn't just for a paycheck. He knew how much the shelter needed him just as he knew how much he needed the shelter. His name was synonymous with Crisis Ministries and he was proud of that.

On Wednesday night I called Fast Company, the moving company where I had applied, to leave a message about any job openings they might have. I knew the office had closed down for the evening, but I hadn't had time throughout the day to call, and besides, putting the bug in Curtis's ear about who I was would set up my follow-up phone call on Thursday. For an additional $2 per hour, I was much more anxious to get a job with them than with the car wash, but it didn't look like it was going to be as easy as John had mentioned at lunch the day before.

On Thursday I was sent out on the same ticket as the day before. More construction cleanup downtown and another $38 in my pocket. Thankfully, it was my last day working for EasyLabor. Every day I went out to work for them, I felt like they were pimping my services. We were working hard, and getting paid peanuts compared to how much EasyLabor was making off of us. Even the peanuts we did earn were whittled away by taxes and fees. I was happy to finally be free from the need to work for the temp agency. My plan was to take Friday and the weekend to prepare to work at the car wash.

Over lunch I had called the office at Fast Company again, but Curtis wasn't in. They gave me his cell phone number, but he didn't pick up my call nor did he return my message back up to the shelter by Thursday night. I was getting the runaround, and there was nothing I could do …

Until I spoke with Phil Coleman on Thursday night over a dinner of spaghetti (yet again!) at the shelter. He had, just as he had promised, landed a job as a landscaper at the Medical University of South Carolina. I congratulated him and told him that it was looking like the car wash was going to be my only option.

"Shiiiiit. Who told you about the car wash? Spike? Shit. That muh' fucka' is the best car washer you're ever gonna meet. He done washed every car in the tri-county area. He's a car washing legend. Made good money, too. Then spent all that money on dope. And look where all that got him. In the bum house, that's where."

I told him that it was looking like it was my only option. I had filled out ten applications and a profile online, and I wasn't getting any response.

"So, hold up a second. Let me get this straight," he said. "You mean to tell me that you live at the homeless shelter, and you have put out over ten applications, and you still don't have a job? What the hell is that all about? Imagine that. That is just craziness, kid." He was not hiding the sarcasm in his voice.

"Man, y'all are some dumb muthas." He began to address the table as a whole, anyone who would listen. "I mean straight dumb asses. How do you think this works? Employers call the number you put on that application and when Harold answers 'Crisis Ministries' they just get real excited that they get to hire a homeless dude? Shit man, y'all some dumb muthas." Choosing that guy to relay my employment woes to was looking like a big mistake. But not quite.

"Listen, y'all muthas gotta change your whole way of thinking. This ain't no fuckin' game. Shit. This is real life. You gotta go down to these managers and be like, 'Look here, homeboy. You need me. I'm the best worker you're gonna find, so hire me or not.' And if it don't work, hell, it don't work. You got like a million other places to go and give the same speech to. Shit, man, it ain't no rocket science. You just gotta go do it. Ha! Do y'all really think they're gonna call here and hire you. Ha! I ain't never heard no shit like that." He started to mumble to himself. "Y'all some dumb muthas."

He had a solid point. Sure, guys were getting hired through the Career Services Department at Crisis Ministries, but I couldn't imagine that many guys were receiving calls at the shelter for applications that they had filled out throughout the city.

Yep, crazy Phil Coleman, a guy that most people ignored, had the secret. Be assertive. That's it. Make the manager see it as a mistake *not* to hire you. "Take me or leave me. Yes? No? I need an answer, cuz, uh, I have another appointment in about fifteen minutes." Something would come along, and when it did, it would be a hell of a lot better than $6.50 an hour. And after I had a job, it was just a matter of disciplining myself enough to keep that job and save the money that I needed to achieve my financial goals.

Scrapping the whole car wash idea altogether and armed with a brand new, Phil Coleman-esque attitude, I had the entire weekend to go out and start schmoozing the managers and owners of any companies I could find.

And Curtis from Fast Company was going to be my first target.

EIGHT

PUT UP OR SHUT UP

⟨◦⟩

The shelter was supposed to be repulsive. That's the only way it could be. It couldn't be comfortable or clean. They couldn't call a plumber every time one of the commodes was out of order or call an electrician to fix a broken light in the hallway. There was a reason Ann and the other shelter employees were stern in their approach to us. There was a reason we didn't have cable TV, and there was a reason that many of our rights and freedoms were checked at the door: they didn't want us there. For our own good, they wanted us out.

Can you imagine how the conversation would go if the shelter was an appealing place to live? Or how many people would come to live there?

"Hey, dude, where do you live?"

"Oh, over there on Meetin' Street. Y'know, at the homeless shelter."

"Oh man. I hear it's nice down there. Very pleasant. I'm thinking about moving there for a few months myself. Y'know, take a little vacation from paying bills and what not."

It's unrealistic for the shelter to be accommodating. Nobody should look forward to living at the shelter. They should come "home" thinking, "Man, I'm sick of this hole. I gotta do something to get out of here."

And, as I was beginning to discover, that was how most of the shelterees felt. While some had become complacent, content with whatever simple pleasures they could find, and others were disgusted yet accepting of the conditions, many longed for the opportunity to be free from the realities of such a dehumanizing world.

Some guys would even make their feelings known, publicly or privately. At breakfast Friday morning, one guy came in with his face all balled up and, without addressing anyone in particular and without providing cause for an outburst, he said, "I hate this place. I hate living here, and I hate all of my roommates."

You can imagine the excitement that ensued in the dining room after that. Everyone started screaming at him at the same time and he was screaming right back at them. They surrounded him like a pack of wild dogs preparing to attack their morning meal. But they never would. Outside the shelter, all bets were off, but inside the shelter, physical confrontation, which was punishable by immediate expulsion from the shelter, was substituted with heated arguments.

Yep, it was another Friday, another great day to do great things. Some people throughout Charleston had already switched their mental buttons to "off" by Friday and couldn't wait for the weekend to really get started, but that wasn't me. Fridays were my day to really make things happen, to get the gears turning.

But this Friday was different. Sure, the birds were chirping and the sun was shining and all that jazz that sets the scene for a red-letter day, but that wasn't it. I felt inherently different. I felt like a new guy, ready to do something worthwhile with my life. Inspired by Phil Coleman's lecture the evening before, I set out that Friday morning with one goal in mind: meet with Curtis McNeil.

I knew that I would get a job that day. I knew it. It might not be at Fast Company as I had hoped, and I might not have a job by lunchtime, but I just knew that I was going to do what it took to get a job that day. I had to. It was Friday!

Of course Curtis wasn't in. *That must be one busy mother,* I thought, when Wendy, receptionist number two of two at Fast Company, politely told me that I could either wait a while or come back later.

I would wait. A "while" or longer, it didn't matter. There was no question that I was going to wait. If the same option came up again at Food Lion or McAllister's Tree Service or Mandy's Tailor, then I would consider leaving and trying my luck at the next spot. But working for Fast Company was something that had piqued my interest, and Curtis was going to get the opportunity to hear what I had to say, a speech that I had been rehearsing in my head since I had laid down on my mattress the night before.

My demeanor was not swayed when he finally did arrive back at the office, noticeably preoccupied with other, much more important business. He walked past where I was sitting and in to see Chris Franklin, the owner. I could overhear him telling Chris about how one of the moving trucks had three busted hinges on the sliding door on the back of the storage van, but Chris didn't seem to want to have anything to do with it.

"Well, let's just get it fixed," he told Curtis.

So Curtis strolled out of Chris's office. And in to see me.

Curtis knew who I was from the messages I had been leaving for him. I was straight with him right from the start, asking if he had any job openings, and he was straight right back with me, telling me that he didn't really need any other movers at the moment. He had my number if any job vacancies came up.

That wasn't going to do. I had been sitting in the office for an hour, waiting for him to return, and I had not been waiting so that I could hear that response. I might be going down, but I wasn't going down without a fight.

"Curtis, my man, I don't want to sit here in front of you and be disrespectful to any of your workers out there, because I'm sure they're all good guys, but, uh, I'm pretty much one of the hardest working guys you're going to find in Charleston. Let me tell you about *the bar*, Curtis. There was no bar before I came along. I set the bar. And I set it high."

He was attentive, totally engrossed in my monologue. And thankfully, he was not mistaking my bit of sarcasm about "the bar" for arrogance. I continued.

"All I want to do is work. I don't drink. I don't smoke. I'm no fun, actually. None of your guys, as great as they may be, have the work ethic that I do. None of 'em. Now, are they better movers? Of course. I mean, you can look at me right here across your desk and tell that I ain't throwin' a sofa over my head and walkin' it off the truck. I mean, let's be honest with each other from the start; that just won't be happening. But I will work hard, and I will pay attention to learn this trade to the best of my ability."

He tried to speak, but I wasn't through yet. My blood was flowing, and my heart was pumping as if it was independent of my body.

"Look here, Curt, wait just a second before you respond." *Curt? Who the hell do I think I am?* "I don't wanna sit here in front of you and act like I'm all talk. Because I'm not. I mean, I'm not gonna lie, I can talk a big game, but I can also back it up. So I'll tell you what. Let's make a deal. You send me out for one day with one of your crews. Any crew. And I'll work for free. You will have the opportunity to see me work, and it won't cost you a dime. If you like me, super, take me on. If not, well, then we will part ways, and I can promise you I won't be a thorn in your ass, coming in here every day begging for a job."

I finished up strong, and then yielded the floor to him.

"Adam, I'm not gonna lie to you, bruh. That's the first time I've heard that speech. Free, huh? Wow. Yeah, that's definitely a first.

That's serious. But that won't even be necessary. I like your attitude. You're hired."

Just like that. For a moment, I thought I was sitting across the desk from Donald Trump and I had just won *The Apprentice*. It was exhilarating. That speech—that cocky, unrehearsed, yet ever-so-eloquent speech—conceived my identity, which I seemed to have been struggling to find during my first ten days in Charleston.

And the most intriguing thing? I didn't even plan it like that! Phil Coleman did. Sure, I would have gotten a job eventually, and I would have fought just as hard to achieve what I had set out to achieve, but my Phil Coleman-esque speech gave me a jump start when I needed it most.

Curtis asked me a series of questions regarding my availability and moving experience.

"I mean, to be honest, Curt, I've moved my parents about five times, but that's about it."

"That's cool," he said. "We'll train you."

"But!" I added, hoping to compensate for my lack of experience. "The good thing is that my hours of availability are infinite. When you need me, I'll be here."

Curtis also inquired about my driving ability. Could I drive a stick? Had I ever driven a moving truck before? Commercial Drivers Licenses were not required to drive the trucks at Fast Company, but some experience driving a truck of that size was recommended. While my pops had, in fact, taught me how to drive a stick when I was in high school, I was going to have to brush up on my truck driving abilities.

So, we went for a test drive. And let me tell you, I took that poor man for the ride of his life. I should have charged him admission. While his facial expressions remained somewhat calm, I know he was shaking in his skivvies. At least I was. Initially, I was most anxious about turning the corners in the big moving truck, but my nemesis turned out to be the stick shift, which was way different from my pop's '95 Ford Escort hatchback. The gears were tighter and the clutch was looser. And since it didn't come with a guide on top of the knob to show which gear was which, I ended up finding first gear by way of elimination after backing into the chain link fence surrounding Fast Company's parking lot.

I tried to fill the fifteen-minute ride with idle small talk, but that just threw me even more off track. I didn't have the mental stamina to drive that truck and talk about anything beyond sports and the beautiful weather. Thankfully, Curt's phone rang twice, and very thankfully, he decided it would be a good time to start answering it. But I still wasn't feeling like I had impressed him enough that he wouldn't renege on hiring me. With the way I had that truck convulsing back and forth as we cruised the back neighborhoods around the airport, I thought our conversation at the end of the test drive would comprise my need to come back for a few lessons before I could start.

But I was wrong. After all was said and done, I had apparently done all right. "All right" meaning Curtis stuck out his hand and told me that I could start on Monday morning.

"I'm going to send you out with Sammy, though," he said. "He's one of the only ones that knows how to drive this truck, so I'll let him teach you."

I was pumped. I pulled the string that served as the door handle, and we headed into the office to take care of the paperwork.

In hindsight, I now realize that my test drive with truck No. 2 was a setup of sorts. Everybody pissed and moaned about driving truck No. 2. As I would later find out, one guy, who was one of the few that knew how to drive a stick, had even quit when they continued to send him out in truck No. 2 despite his repeated requests to be assigned to another truck once in a while. Maybe Curtis saw me as somebody that he could finally stick on truck No. 2, but I didn't care. *Put me in whatever truck you want and send me wherever you want.* I was tickled pink just to have a job. And, at $9 an hour! Adding even more excitement to my afternoon, Curtis informed me that drivers started out at $1 above the rate that regular movers made. I was psyched. I was well aware that I had chosen a very demanding occupation when I chose to become a mover, and I certainly knew that I had plenty to learn about my new job and driving big trucks and the like, but I was ready for it. I was ready for whatever Fast Company had in store for me.

As much as I would have loved to have returned to the shelter amid encouraging toasts of congratulations for getting hired by the moving company, it was an announcement that I very astutely reserved for the select few people that I had come to know pretty well during my short stay at the shelter. While it was true that many people would surely be happy that I got a job, they would also harbor a bit of jealousy at the fact that they remained unemployed. I didn't want to create any uncomfortable feelings. Besides, they would find out sooner or later anyway. I did, however, seek out Phil Coleman to thank him for his pep talk the night before.

"Shit, ain't nothin', kid," he said, shrugging his shoulders and raising his eyebrows. "Now we just gotta hold on to these jobs."

Friday also marked the day that I started to see Omar on a more sporadic basis. For the two months that I lived at the shelter, my experience with Omar was always up and down. *Which Omar is going to show up today?* One day, he would arrive at the shelter for dinner, full of life, talking about his ambitions and how we had to get an apartment together, and the next day he would be distant, as if he didn't even really know what was worth aiming for anymore. More often than not, I could see where he was coming from. He was bummed about living at the shelter. He hated it. He tried to stay out as often as possible with friends or girls who he'd met along the way. And who could blame him? The atmosphere at the shelter had a way of dragging people down. Sure, we were there for each other, some of us cheering on the next guy as he sought a better situation, but that didn't do much for the overall disposition at the shelter. The fact remained that we were conscious of our standing as homeless men, the filth on the bottom floor of life's social structure.

I spent the weekend preparing myself to begin work on Monday. On Sunday, I continued what would become tradition in working for George downtown. Some Sundays he would only assign me two or three hours of work, and other Sundays, he would have a list that would take me six hours to complete. But every Sunday, I didn't start working until at least 11:00 AM as George would rise late, groggy-eyed from the previous night's leisure activities. That second Sunday that I worked for him, he had me continue to pull weeds from the same rocky foundation on which I had worked before. The work that I did for George was always tedious and lacking excitement, and the sun always shone directly on my back throughout the entire day, but it always came with a fat $10-an-hour paycheck.

On Sunday evening at the shelter, I had a very illuminating conversation with Leo, the guy who had followed the woman from Los Angeles only to surprisingly confront her husband when he got here. He was very down to earth and had a good head on his shoulders. He saw his stay at Crisis Ministries—as brief as it was—as more of an adventure than a way of life, an opportunity to see a part of the United States that he hadn't seen before. He had even toyed with the idea of staying on the East Coast for a bit, but said that it wasn't nearly as exciting as life on the left side.

"I know a lotta stuff, Shep. I mean a lot. I'm working with genius capabilities. That's prolly why my head is so damn big: it's jam-packed with knowledge. Humble? Not so much. Savvy? Absolutely. Let me tell you a little bit about what I know about society as a whole.

"There are three kinds of people, and I'm not talking about just in the shelter. I'm talking about in general, three kinds of people." He told me the three kinds of people are: those that go to school and educate themselves and go on to live professional lives; workaholics, who spend their entire lives breaking their backs, laboring to make somebody else rich; and the lazy, those people that don't do anything with their lives. They crawl from job to job, paycheck to paycheck, somehow finding satisfaction in scraping by.

"I don't have a problem with the first two," he said. "They're making an honest living. But those lazy people? They're ridiculous. They piss me off. They're up to no good. And the worst part is that they drain the life out of everybody else.

"I'll give you an example," he continued. "You ever seen crabs in a pot? When one of them climbs to the top to try to get out, all the other crabs grab him and pull him back in. Misery loves company. That's what I'm talkin' about."

He went on to explain his view that we live in a society that allows everyone the freedom to do what he or she wants with his or her life. "If you want to make something of yourself, you can do it," he said. Conversely, if you want to be a bum, you have the freedom to be a bum. America allows us that choice.

"But, you also gotta understand something, Shep," he continued. "Some of the people in the lower class start out behind. We all have the same freedoms, true, but those of us born into poverty don't necessarily have the guidance." He told me that many people are not fortunate to grow up with two loving parents and a backyard and somewhere to go after school. They grow up on sketchy sides of town, and their social activities are limited to whatever their friends are doing after school, which usually aren't very legitimate activities.

"But, I'll tell you this," he said. "There comes a time for everybody that it's time to grow up. I mean, look at me. I came from a broken home. Mama's got six kids. No daddy. Maybe the lights will turn on today; maybe not. Eatin' mayonnaise and pickle sandwiches. I started out less fortunate than most people, and I lived my life accordingly. Streets, drugs, violence ... all that. But then I turned twenty and realized that it was time to shape up or I would be in prison or dead just like everybody else I knew."

Leo loved talking just as much as I loved listening. And he really loved using big words. He would add extra emphasis whenever he would say a word like *irreverent* or *eradicated* and his eyes would light up with delight, as if to say, "Yeah, *eradicated*. That's exactly what happened. It got eradicated. Man, I'm smart."

It was appealing to meet some of those people at the shelter. Sure, Crisis Ministries had its fair share of laggards and old, bearded men with whiskey on their breath, just like the hobos I had imagined, but what about the other guys like Omar and James and Rico and Easy E, who had been dealt a crappy hand of cards, but really, genuinely cared about getting their life back in the right direction? While I had anticipated meeting a wide variety of people and confronting all kinds of attitudes, it was still a bit of a surprise to meet guys like them, just as it was a huge surprise to attain lessons in social science from Leo, who never finished the tenth grade. I wondered—and would never draw a definitive conclusion—why a guy like Leo could be so well-grounded, while other guys were lazy or had given up, many from the same hopeless circumstances and all with a different attitude.

So, there it was. It had taken me ten days, but I had a job, and I was finally to the point where I could rest easy. True, I had less than a hundred bucks in my pocket, but I had the job for which I had been anxiously awaiting. While the argument could be made that my project had only just begun, I knew that time was the only thing standing between my goals and me. Discipline and patience would get me there. As I laid my head on my sleeping bag's built-in inflatable pillow that Sunday night, with the restlessness of a five-year-old preparing for his first day of kindergarten running through me, I prepared myself for the leisurely part of my project: working and saving money.

Then again, if you know anything about moving furniture, you know that my life was going to be anything but leisurely.

NINE

"FIRST AND LAST DAY"

❦

For my first twelve days in Charleston, I had been carrying all of my belongings with me in the gym bag that I had brought to begin my journey. It was starting to be a hassle, but there wasn't much else I could do. During one of my first days at the shelter, I tried to leave my belongings on top of the lockers while I worked my way around town, but Ann confiscated my bag. I got my bag back, but not without a fierce scolding. "Next time, it's mine," she said, her eyes slant. "For keeps." That lady was an animal.

So on Monday morning, I checked back with her for about the fifth time to see if she had any lockers available yet. And she did. So for $1 a week I rented my own personal space where I could keep my valuables—which weren't necessarily valuable—safe throughout the day.

Some days the shelter served as a labor agency of its own. Guys would stand around the shelter yard waiting for someone to come by soliciting the help of two guys to help load a U-Haul or do yard chores or paint. People knew they could get cheap labor from the guys at the shelter just as the guys at the shelter were more than willing to work any cash job they could find. In fact, a few guys made pretty good money doing that every day. And if no one had come by to pick them up by nine or 9:30, they would walk to the open-air market downtown to help the merchants unload goods from their cars and vans for $10 a pop. They could make $20 or $30 in the morning and then double their wad in the late afternoon by helping the merchants load the goods back in their cars. And during their few hours off, they could panhandle or take a nap. It was a pretty cavalier lifestyle.

By the time I had figured out how those guys were earning extra cash, I already had a permanent job. The No. 10 bus came at 6:15 AM and every half hour after that for the remainder of the day. I would catch the bus, travel thirty minutes up Rivers Avenue, get off, and walk a quarter-mile along the train tracks. From there, it was a hundred-yard jaunt through the woods to get to the Fast Company office. On my first trip through the woods, I nearly stepped on a three-foot snake resting in the grass, but it didn't deter me from committing to take that same route every day. Maybe I couldn't tell the difference between a copperhead and a garter snake, but it was still worth the risk. As far as time and economy were concerned, I had come across the most efficient system. And since I had stopped by the bus system's headquarters on Thursday to get my discount bus card—for which anyone with low income was eligible—I could ride the bus for just fifty cents each way.

I decided to take the 6:45 bus. That would get me at Fast Company just before 7:30 AM and well before Curtis's required eight o'clock arrival time. If I could show them that I was willing to be early, and do whatever else they asked of me, it would more than likely lead to my rise in the ranks of the hierarchy of movers and perhaps lead to assignments on better moves.

At least that's what I hoped after I saw the first move to which I was assigned. One bedroom, one living room, one dining room. Piece of cake. Two-story house to an apartment on the third floor. Hmmmm.

That added a little flavor to the cake.

"Old Man Jimmy," the fifty-six-year-old Fast Company legend who had been moving furniture since he was thirteen and had trained all of the movers at Fast Company that were any good, looked over my move and made an outright declaration: "First and last day! Everybody see the young buck here? Today is his first and last day."

One bedroom was no problem. One living room? One dining room? No sweat. But, the second floor is no joke when it comes to hauling furniture. The third floor, especially on your first day, is suicide. Everybody laughed when Old Man Jimmy made the announcement, but I didn't say anything. I just smiled right along with them. Those steps didn't stand a chance at beating me. I had been waiting for the first day of my new job since I arrived in Charleston, and nothing was going to get in my way.

Fast Company, which specializes in local moves within the Charleston area but also services out-of-town moves throughout the entire Southeast, has a revolutionary way of charging for their moves, a system that has been copied by other moving companies over the years. Two men are sent out on the smaller jobs at a rate of $89 per hour plus a one-time $89 travel charge. For the bigger moves, a third man is sent out for an additional $21 per hour. This saves the company the hassle of having to go out on estimates, and it gives the customer a pretty good idea of how much their move will cost. With other moving companies charging by the piece or by weight, on-site estimates became a burden, and even then, there's no telling how much their move could total. Charging by the hour was efficient for everybody.

More importantly, as I would find out, Fast Company had built their reputation by not only being safe and inexpensive, but also, as the name implies, being the fastest company in town.

For my first day, I was assigned to work with Sammy and Bruno. While most of the thirty-two movers at Fast Company worked on permanent crews, Sammy and Bruno chose to come in and work with different people every day. They knew that it would give them a better chance of going out on a consistent basis, and, contrary to others' preferences, they didn't care who they were sent out with.

Although short, my first day at Fast Company did not go by without excitement. Curtis had instructed Sammy to let me drive, putting me behind the wheel in a walk-before-you-crawl type situation.

"He's not gonna learn how to drive that thing from the passenger side," Curtis announced. "Might as well go ahead and let him get his feet wet."

Which was fine with me. I had always been an active learner: more do, less watch. I had come out of the womb jumping rope and reciting times tables, so I figured I was ready for anything. Unfortunately, however, to my passengers' dismay, it turned out that I was a slow learner when it came to driving moving trucks. Expectations were low, and I wasn't even meeting those. I was tripping over "the bar" that I had so pompously told Curtis I had set. There was nothing I could do. Believe me, I wanted to be a good driver. I'm a perfectionist, and I hate when I'm slow to catch on to things. But that truck No. 2 was an enigma. I would have rather worked on solving the Rubik's Cube blindfolded. I knew right away it was going to take a while to get the hang of driving that truck. Whereas riders on the other trucks could sit back and relax on the way to and from their moves, our situation for that first day was different. Bruno took the window seat and control of the radio, while Sammy, with his long legs, squeezed in the middle and kept a very attentive eye on the road, constantly requesting that I go "just a little slower around the curves" or "maybe move a little bit more on this side of the double yellow line."

I wasn't embarrassed, though. Well, that's a lie. Yes I was. While they knew beforehand what they were getting into with my inexperience, and even with Sammy's upbeat, understanding attitude, I still felt so unfit to be driving that truck.

But things started to look up when we got to the move. First of all, the young lady we moved was beautiful. Gorgeous. Shannon

O'Bannon. I'll never forget that name—one of those names that makes you want to dance and sing, maybe sit down and write a nursery rhyme. Which, in fact, Bruno was doing in between trips in and out of the house.

Shannon O'Bannon had a fat fanny,
whose rumps were soft as dough.
Everywhere that Shannon went,
the boys were sure to go ...

She was twenty-five, younger than the typical Fast Company customer and was already divorcing her husband, whom she had caught cheating.

"That mother fucker." She pepped up real quick. "I hired one of those private investigators like you see on TV, and we installed cameras and microphones all over the place. We followed him around in the undercover van for three days. I got that bastard good."

Well, that explained the cheating, but she was still beautiful. My first thought when we arrived at the move was that if I got to wake up and look forward to moving people like her, then my job might not be so bad after all.

Shannon O'Bannon also didn't have a lot of stuff, which was another perk on my first job. She was moving out of the house and into her own one-bedroom apartment. She had moved all of the little things herself—a concept that some customers understood saved them time and money—so we just had to get the big items. We cleared the upstairs bedroom and then moved out all of the dining room and living room furniture from downstairs. Sammy and Bruno were shaking a leg. They were much less interested in teaching me how to move furniture than getting to Shannon's third-floor apartment and getting the job over with.

"You gonna grab something heavy, lanky?" Bruno joked. I think.

They had me loading nightstands and side tables onto the truck, while they "two-manned" the sofas and dressers. Which I didn't mind. I would have plenty of time to pick up the tricks of the trade as time passed.

In an hour we had everything loaded up and we headed over to Shannon's new place, twenty minutes away in West Ashley. As dramatic as I could make the unload sound, it wasn't. Sure, it was the third floor, but we had three guys, and she didn't even have that many pieces of furniture. Her bulky sleeper sofa was a chore to lug up the stairs and through her front door, but we got that out of the way early so everything else was rather simple. It took an hour to unload the truck and take care of the bill. She tipped us $25 for the three of us to split.

If there was one good thing that I discovered I had going for me as a mover, it was that I didn't stop. Sure, I wasn't terribly strong, and I didn't really know how to use the dollies to my advantage when carting furniture to and fro, but that didn't necessarily matter to Sammy and Bruno. I kept going and they loved me for that. Maybe it took me an extra moment or two to get the right grip on a dresser, but I could carry my end of it up the stairs, and as soon as we placed it in the apartment, I skipped back down to pick up another piece.

"Shoot, man, take a break every now and then," Sammy would say.

But I couldn't. It's how I had always worked. Not that I was some tough kid with something to prove, showing that I had what it took. It wasn't that at all. It was just that I knew that as soon as I took a break, it was all uphill from there. I would become lethargic. I would start dragging. I wouldn't be able to get back to the same pace as before. Once I started, I had to keep going until the truck was empty or I would be no good.

So, in the end, I survived my first day of my new career as a professional mover. It was my last day with Sammy, though. Drivers worked together only on rare occasions when Fast Company was short on moves, but Sammy would be gone before we would have that opportunity. Curse of truck No. 2.

We arrived back at the shop around noon, and I told Curtis that we had a great day and that I was very grateful to have the opportunity to work for Fast Company.

"You got another one-bedroom tomorrow," he told me. I was assigned to work with another guy who didn't have a permanent crew.

While I would have to really prove myself before I could go to work on a big, three- or four-bedroom move, it was a great feeling to know that I could get into a routine. Wake up, hop on the bus, and go to work. Maybe I would work until 11 AM or maybe I wouldn't be off until later in the afternoon if the job turned out to be bigger than the moving sheet said. Either way, it didn't matter. I didn't have a schedule to adhere to. As long as I was working and staying at the shelter, I could stay out of trouble and on course to complete my mission.

What was I going to do with the rest of my day, though? If some of my moves were going to be completed by noon, I was going have to figure out what to do with the balance of my time. The shelter didn't open up until 7:30, and I refused to be a member of the gang of guys that sat in the shelter yard all day long waiting for check-in time.

So I would head to the bottom of the downtown peninsula and search for things to do. Simple things. Anything that didn't cost money. I was easy to please, and that alone alleviated the distress of what others might consider a disgraceful social life, which was resigned to trips to the bookstore and the library with Larry, walks downtown by the waterfront and through historic neighborhoods, and window-shopping along King Street's long line of trendy shops. On the weekends at Marion Square, there was always free entertainment, parades, or special events like the Budweiser Clydesdale exhibit. I had made a commitment—or perhaps the commitment had been made for me by default—that my social life would suffer as I fought to achieve my goals. Interesting to me, though, was the fact that it wasn't a difficult commitment to make nor was it a difficult commitment to keep. I knew what I had to do to get where I wanted to go, and I knew that late nights partying with the beautiful, busty girls I saw on a daily basis downtown could cost me in so many ways. So I remained focused on the task at hand.

But don't get my intentions twisted. Did I want to go to Club Habana or Wet Willie's or any one of the other nightclubs I had walked past, places where I could dance and party all evening long with the chicks from the College of Charleston? Damn right! Weren't the comedy shows and plays appealing to me as they were for others in my peer group? Sure, but I knew they weren't a smart investment. Perhaps a time would come for all of that. In fact, ideas like that kept me motivated. Work hard, play hard. Knowing that one day I would have the time and resources to do so many other things with my life kept me getting up every day to do what was absolutely necessary for me to advance.

Not that any girls would have wanted to hang out with me though. It's crazy how we become the product of our surroundings. Early on, even after just two weeks into my project, I began to see myself transform. I started not to care what I dressed like or looked like. I started saying "I ain't sure" and "Yeah, I done heard about that." Without even thinking twice about it. While I was walking down the street, I would pick my nose and scratch between my legs. I'm sure I was quite the sight to strangers walking by, but I didn't care. I was in my own world. I was invincible. I had more confidence than a room full of Tony Robbins's greatest disciples. Nothing could stop me.

Now, don't get me wrong here. I'm not saying that I went into the homeless shelter and thought, "Welp, now I can pick my nose and scratch myself and I'll blend in." Not everybody exhibited those habits. Most of us, but not everybody. What I'm saying is that there was one of two ways that I could go with my newly adopted fearlessness: A) I could sit around and fall into a funk, or B) I could use it to channel my advancement. And I chose the latter. I really let go of all suppression.

I wasn't concerned with what everybody else was doing or with what they thought about me. My life was a blank canvas, and I had the freedom to create whatever kind of masterpiece I wanted to create. The confidence that came with having nowhere to go but up gave me the opportunity to really just let loose and be myself. And that was one of the greatest feelings I had ever experienced.

It was funny, too, how different people had different views of the shelter. When I would work with George on Sunday, he would lower his voice and look around and say things like, "So, you still stayin' over there at the, y' know, the shelter?" Ha. "Yeah, man. I'm still there. And you don't have to treat it like it is so taboo." Conversely, I would be riding the bus and a shelter mate sitting across from me would holler something, without even caring who was listening, like, "Hey, Shep, whatchya think we're gonna have for dinner tonight at the shelter? I hope it's Robert's meatloaf. His meatloaf is God-damned out of sight." We didn't care what people thought. We were walking our own made up fine line with absolutely no pride left on one side and an overabundance of pride on the other.

Which, of course, didn't mean we weren't hungrier every day to get the heck out of that place. Truthfully, I could have made plans to move out of the shelter pretty soon after I had landed a job, just like Larry was doing with the two-bedroom apartment that he was planning to move into the following Friday. One-bedroom apartments with the Housing Authority—where a lot of homeless guys made their transition—were $150 down and thirty percent of one's paycheck per month or I could rent a room from "Honest John," who worked at the corner Quickie Mart, for $95 down and $95 a week, cash. Either would be a feasible first step out of the shelter, a step that many people from the shelter were making, but it wasn't exactly what I wanted to be doing. I wanted something more concrete and certainly something more secure. The area around the shelter represented an environment that seemed to prevent progress rather than promote it. The year before my arrival in Charleston, *The Post and Courier* reported that a group of local gangsters had used a housing project right around the corner from the shelter as one of the backdrops in a homemade rap music video. They carried assault rifles and showcased drugs and heaps of cash in the presence of children that appeared to be younger than ten. The lyrics of their music exhibited their rebellion against the police and their unwillingness to obey the law. The DVD, which became infamous almost immediately after its publication, became a great investigative tool for local police and led to the arrests of many of the men that appeared on screen, most of whom already had outstanding warrants. It was big news for a year. Yeah, the area around the shelter was exciting, no doubt, but not the kind of excitement I was looking for. The whole point of what I was doing was to crawl my way out of that lifestyle, so I planned to hold out for a better situation.

So I resolved to stay at the shelter as long as I needed to, until I could find a secure place to live either by myself or with Omar.

But Omar still wasn't showing his face very often at the shelter. In fact, I hadn't seen Omar since Friday, and I wouldn't see him again for two more weeks after I started my job. I would come home to the shelter after work every day with high hopes that he would show up, and every night my hopes would be shot down. I would literally watch the door for him to come home. I was a dog waiting for his master to return. I missed that guy. A lot. I mean, I'd only known him a short time, but he was already working his way into being an integral part of my life. As independent as I tried to believe I was, the truth was that I needed Omar. This wasn't *my* story, *my* project. This was *our* project. Adam and Omar's story. A companion like Omar would make my life so much more livable, especially since we had connected on so many levels, and, most importantly, we had a plan. I felt like he was letting me down, like he didn't care about me or our plans or what we could accomplish together. I began to realize that maybe he was all talk.

But I did my best not to think about that. Besides, I had plenty to keep me entertained. Like TV. Although I appreciated film, I had never been much of a television watcher. I would watch it if it was on or if there was some special event or maybe there was a show that I would really get into for a month, but I was always so busy with other pursuits. In the confined world of the shelter, though, the television was one of the things that kept us amused and connected to life elsewhere.

There was no question that *COPS* was everybody's favorite show. No doubt about it. At 8:00 PM, when *COPS* appeared on one of the two channels that came in with minimal static, everyone in the shelter crowded around. It was routine. Everybody was loud and obnoxious during dinner, but when *COPS* came on, we all fell silent. There was important business to tend to.

But we didn't watch TV's original reality show like I used to when I was a kid. Growing up, I used to love watching that show so that I could see what idiots there were around the nation and find satisfaction in the fact that no matter how crazy I thought I was, I was more stable than those people.

Nope. We watched it in a completely different light. We cheered for the suspected criminal the whole way through. It didn't matter what the accusations were, and it didn't matter who was on the other end. We always cheered for the guy the cops were after. Guys would be huddled around the TV set, hollering, "Go mother fucker! Shit. Go! Hop that fence! Go! Go! Ah. Ah. Ah, damn, they got 'im. Again. They got 'im again. He shoulda hopped that fence like I said. Damn. They always get 'im." And they would always give the criminal the benefit of the doubt. After a long chase, the cops would dig in the suspected criminal's pockets and find some illicit drug or whatever and the guys at the shelter would look around at each other and murmur, "Shit, that's bullshit. You know that's bullshit. They planted that on him. He ain't have that on him before. They put it there. So their stupid TV show can get ratings." And they were serious, too. Every night we would watch, every night we would pull for the criminal, and every night he would be dragged away in handcuffs.

But we didn't always need the television for entertainment. Somebody was always around to stimulate our attention. If it wasn't one guy creating mischief around the shelter, it was another guy. Every night there was something new. It was great. And once one guy got going, it was easy for everybody else to follow suit. We would have some of the most intriguing debates I'd ever been a part of. Sometimes intellectual, sometimes philosophical, sometimes political, but always insightful. And everybody always had at least his two cents to put in. Usually more. Even guys who normally remained silent and in their own world would offer their input from time to time. I can remember one night we were talking about the war in Iraq, a frequent topic of conversation. We were going back and forth on the various issues knowing that none of us were necessarily right and that nobody was going to change anybody else's mind. Then this guy, Davey Dizzle, who sat, ate, and then slept in the same corner every night and said about two words per day and never bothered a soul, said, "You know what we need to do? We need to just drop a God-damned bomb on all them mothers and call it a day." We all just looked at each other in absolute puzzlement, I'm talking almost terrified, like, *Wait a sec? Dizzle? Did Dizzle just speak? And did he just say that we should drop a bomb on all of 'em and call it a day?* Even Brian Brizzle—Davey's twin brother and the resident loudmouth—had a shocked look plastered on his face. We all sat there for a moment, speechless, and let it sink in before we picked up our discussion right where we had left off. But the point had been made: everybody had a voice at the shelter.

And most guys didn't wait for their turn to speak. They would just come over to you and start a conversation. Guys like Mustafa Frederick. If there is one person from the shelter that I will never forget, he's the one. He was the kindest, gentlest young man that I met at the shelter and probably during my entire stay in Charleston. He was about 5'4" and his muscles were chiseled like those on a statue of an ancient Greek god. He always walked around shirtless and he was always doing some form of physical activity. He was respectful to everyone, no matter who it was, and everybody was respectful right back to him. You never would have guessed that he had spent three of his twenty-seven years in prison.

And he was eccentric. Super-eccentric. He always had something fun and new and, most importantly, absolutely insane to talk about. One time he came up to me and told me what he knew about the barracuda. He said something like, "Hey, Gabriel ..." (he called me Gabriel, because he said I reminded him of one of the archangels in the Bible) "... did you know that a barracuda is actually a combination of a fish and a dragon and a hawk? Right now, it can only exhibit its fish powers, because the other two are chained down by the demons deep below the Earth's surface, but believe me, one day, the barracuda is going to take over the world."

What? I mean, seriously, what? What was he talking about? I didn't know. Hell, nobody knew! And we loved it. Anytime Mustafa wanted to add commentary, he was given the floor. Automatically, no questions asked. His remarks usually ended with us either grabbing our bellies in laughter or looking around at each other in absolute disbelief. For me, it was usually both. And he loved it. He loved being the center of attention.

Mustafa and I always talked. He would tell me about his tough times in prison and what he did to relieve the dreariness of everyday life. He became very spiritual throughout his time behind bars (for which he would never reveal his crime). At night in his cell, he clogged the sink, filled it with water, and soaked his Bible. In the morning, he ripped out a page and drained the water into his mouth. The holy water, he said, kept his mind clear while he was incarcerated and enabled him the freedom to be mindful of the evils that got him locked up in the first place. And that's when I realized that there was some merit behind his insanity. Sure, he had some crazy ideas running around in his head, but ironically, that is what kept him mentally sound and out of trouble. His insanity kept him in touch with normalcy. In his crazy little world, he was able to distinguish right from wrong. So who were we to say what a barracuda was or wasn't or call him a nut for soaking his Bible in holy water when that was what was keeping him from making the poor decisions that had landed him in prison in the first place?

It also turned out that Mustafa's natural ability to entertain was not limited to the shelter. He would stand down at the corner of Columbus and Meeting Street in front of the Piggly Wiggly throughout the day, every day, preaching. He wouldn't ask for money and he didn't pose a threat. He was just there, speaking to anyone that would listen. No one could be certain of the topic of his sermons, but I can promise you it was eye opening. Passersby would cross his path, pausing to listen to his far-out words of wisdom, and then walk off with a snicker, far more puzzled than they had been before. After repeated inquiries about his identification and purpose, the local newspaper did a full spread on him while I was still in the shelter, but it didn't do any justice to the real identity of Mustafa Frederick. That guy was one of a kind.

Sarge didn't show up on Monday night and the rumor spread quickly from person to person around the shelter that he had been gunned down on the street a la John Wayne, when in fact, he was in the hospital after suffering a heart attack. Either way, a few guys were excited to be free from his constraint for a few days, but the shelter veterans knew that he would probably be back the next day. And he was. I heard he'd even checked himself out of the hospital Arnold Schwarzenegger style—just ripped the wires and tubes off his body and walked out of his room—but nobody really knew if that was fact or fallacy. I just knew that all of the rumors running around spoke of Sarge's reputation at the shelter.

And I knew that he was back. "Ha! Sarge's gonna die in this place,

I'm tellin' you," one guy said. "Literally. Here at the shelter. On this floor right here. He's gonna keel over and die, work himself to death." And he was probably right. Sarge's passion shone through every night as I began to wonder if the guys at the shelter truly appreciated what Sarge did or if he was just another security guard to them. Either way, I was grateful to go to bed every night with the assurance that I was protected from the people outside just as I was protected from the people on the inside. If he wasn't getting any appreciation, he was certainly getting plenty of respect. Most everybody knew that Sarge got his kicks from removing troublesome characters from the shelter. Some would try him by starting a scuffle or smoking in a bathroom stall (a felony in the shelter!), and those guys would earn the right to spend the night either under the stars or in a jail cell.

If nothing else, living in Sarge's world by Sarge's rules made people seek creative means of vengeance. I can remember one night, late in my stay at the shelter, when two guys were arguing about a sleeping spot. A new guy had checked in and occupied the sleeping space of a guy who had been staying at the shelter for quite some time. The new guy was raising a ruckus about the fact that there were no assigned sleeping spots ("It says so right here on the *Shelter Rules and Regulations*"), so he was going to remain where he was. The shelter veteran just stood there and said, "Okay, fair enough." We all knew that wouldn't be the end of it. So, when the new guy hit the showers, the veteran went to the dining room and grabbed all of the tables and chairs and stacked them in the new guy's sleeping area. I'm talking to the ceiling. The new guy was pissed off big time when he got back from the showers, and he actually ended up getting sent out for the night when he wouldn't calm down. The veteran felt so content with his retaliation that he didn't even mind sleeping in another spot for the night.

Some guys, though, didn't care if they got kicked out of the shelter. As a matter of fact, some guys actually preferred to live Odare.

"Odare?"

"Odare under the bridge! Ha! Man, that never gets old." I heard that at least fifteen times while I lived in the shelter. It got old.

One of the guys that I had met at the mass baptism, whose path I would cross quite often at the library, was convinced that if you could learn how to survive on the streets, it was better (even safer, he felt) and certainly more liberating than staying at the shelter.

"Ain't nuttin' like sleepin' outside, lookin' up 'er at the Big Dipper," he told me.

To each his own, I suppose.

Yeah, there was plenty of excitement to keep me occupied, but all I needed to keep my mind at peace was Fast Company. No matter what happened or what kind of stress I encountered, it was important that I went to work every morning with a smile on my face and a hop in my step, which wasn't that difficult to do. While it surely wasn't easy to get amped up about hauling dressers and boxes around all day, I was energized by the idea that my time as a mover, however long it may be, was finite. Every day led me one more step in the right direction, and that was right where I wanted to be.

TEN

ADVENTURE IN MOVING

❦

L ife is bracing, with all of its peaks and valleys.
By day four of my new job, I had already been assigned a permanent
partner to work with. I had my very own crew.

Shaun Caldwell was atypical of most of the movers at Fast
Company and unquestionably my exact opposite. He was thirty-nine
years old, short, loud-mouthed, cocky, and very much in control. He
had one of those walks in which he strutted from side to side and
swung his arms back and forth—a walk that made you think twice
as he was approaching you about how much money you owed him
or what you may have done wrong to cross him. But, while he meant
business in everything he did, he was also very likable and enjoyable
to talk to. Some of the guys at the shop questioned his habits, but they
all loved socializing with him in the office in the morning before we
would go out on a move.

And his driver had very conveniently resigned on Wednesday, just
two days after my start at Fast Company.

The first thing we would do every morning around eight o'clock on our way to the move (and the habit that kept many people from wanting to work with him) was stop by the gas station around the corner for his "spinach." With his spinach, he was juiced up, his senses were magnified, and he could move anything. But without it, he was cranky and irritable and difficult to be around. His spinach cost $1.09 (times two or three on most days) and came in twenty-four-ounce cans with the words "Natural Light" printed on the outside. After we made the stop, he would hop back in the truck, crack open the top, and proclaim, every time, "Come to papa!" Every day. I would drive, he would drink, and together we would move furniture with such speed that it appeared that we had somewhere more important to be. It was a ritual we established early on.

And I didn't mind. How could I? As long as he was pulling his own weight—literally and figuratively—I didn't care what he was doing. I did mention once or twice that it was incredible that he could drink beer and still be capable of being such a beast, but all he could say was that he was so used to it that it didn't phase him anymore. Besides, by his own acknowledgment, he wasn't even one of the better movers at the company. Among the history of Fast Company that he would offer from time to time, he told me who the big dogs at the company were: "JB, Jody, Mike, Derrick. Dem da beasts uh da company. Can't nobody move like dem."

As impressed as I was with Shaun's strength and efficiency, I could only imagine what it would be like to work with one of those other four guys—guys who would pick up a sofa, throw it on their back, and carry it to the front door, and then come back out for the next piece. I was hoping that one day I would get the chance to see them in action, but it was a long shot. Even with the heart of a lion, it was enough of a challenge for me to carry my end of a washing machine with Shaun, so how was I ever going to be respectable enough to go on a move with those guys?

In the meantime, Shaun was teaching me the ropes, how to use the box dolly, the four-wheeler, and "Big Red" to my advantage, saving my back from lifting every piece. He also taught me Fast Company's unique way of wrapping furniture. Most other moving companies carried the piece out and wrapped a pad around it on the truck, but not us. All leather and wood and any other piece that was scratchable or breakable was covered with a pad and then shrink wrapped to the piece. Shrink wrap, in all of its universal glory, has infinite uses. In addition to using it for wrapping furniture, we were using it to keep our pants up, as door handles on the truck, and to keep the side view mirrors from blowing in the wind when a bolt fell off. We could use it for anything. It was miraculous. It's the new duct tape. Sometimes, though, shrink-wrapping the furniture was just as hard, if not harder, than carrying the piece out the door. We would have these big, industrial-sized rolls of shrink wrap that we would wind around every crevice of the piece, a dizzying chore, ensuring that the pad stayed on until we ripped the shrink wrap off at the customer's new house. While it could be considered time consuming (an additional minute per piece), the process easily made up for itself as it worked to everybody's benefit. It made the piece easier to transport, and it made it easier for us to stack in the truck. And the customers felt more comfortable knowing that we weren't going to scratch their furniture. There was plenty more damage that we could do (like tripping and dropping mirrors or crashing into walls), but scratching the furniture was something that we were able to avoid by wrapping it the way we did.

The differences between Shaun and I positively worked in our favor every day, in every way. He would come into the office and demand that we be put on the better moves. With his aggressive style, we would find ourselves heading to Mount Pleasant (the posh area east of the Cooper River) nearly every day. If we weren't on a good move, then he would talk to Curtis or his boss, Pam, and get it switched. "Naw, naw. This here ain't gonna work, boss lady. We'll take that one, though," he would say. Best of all, he wouldn't back down until he was satisfied. We were always in the shop at least a half hour before all of the other small timers, so we pretty much got the pick of any small job that we wanted. By the time they would get there, we would be long gone. It wasn't really that serious, though. Any of the guys that really cared in the first place were going out on bigger moves anyway and didn't pay any attention to Shaun and me.

Our differences also worked to our advantage on the moves. I was sociable and cordial, quizzing customers on where they were from, what they did for a living, and the like. For the most part, Shaun would steer clear of social interaction with the customer, yielding all of his energy my way in letting me know that my future as a mover looked bleak. Then, at the conclusion of the move, just as I would be settling the bill, he would march in and address the customer, saying something to the effect of, "So! Guess what time it is! It's tippy tip time!" or "You know what a little birdie just told me? He told me that you're the big-shot tipper around these parts." Although it could sometimes be misconstrued as condescending or disrespectful (since a tip was supposed to be an added bonus and never expected), that was not his intention. He kept the mood light, and we were always grateful for the tips we received, whether it was $10 or $50, but I can only imagine that his added quips meant more dollars for us in the long run.

In the early weeks, Shaun was enjoyable to work with. Although I never divulged the premise of my project, I felt comfortable enough to offer him bits of truth about where I had come from. Our contrasting backgrounds left us with plenty to talk about. My father received his M.B.A. from George Washington University, worked as an economic developer for the North Carolina Department of Commerce, and taught me how to throw a curve ball. Shaun's dad served the country in the armed forces and taught him how to kill a man with a toothbrush—not something that Shaun was particularly proud of, but a mastered skill nonetheless. I grew up playing sports and reading whatever I could get my hands on, while Shaun spent his younger years on the streets, fighting and hustling dope. I went to college. Shaun served a seven-year sentence at Sing-Sing in upstate New York for manslaughter, a story that we revisited as often as he wanted to talk about it. It was a typical gangster story, like the ones you pay $9 to see at Carmike Cinemas.

He was at a nightclub in New York, hanging out with a few friends. They were drinking and dancing and having a good time. One of the guys he was with was celebrating his birthday, so Shaun's friend had ordered up the VIP treatment—corner booth, expensive champagne, and girls. Plenty of girls. Guys around the club started to get a little jealous and came over to talk to them about it. A fight ensued, one of the guys pulled a knife, and Shaun was stabbed three times in his stomach area. One of the scars he showed me was at least three inches long on the side of his body. It was a miracle that he survived, he told me. He was laid up in the hospital for two months while doctors performed several surgeries. While he was out of commission, his brother asked around and found out who had stabbed Shaun and where he could be found. When Shaun got out of the hospital, he popped him.

The State of New York evidently has aggressive plea bargain opportunities, and Shaun said the District Attorney also took it a little easy on him since he had been stabbed first. He was sentenced to ten years and served seven.

But Shaun's demeanor didn't present him as a felon. Most of the other guys that I had met along the way and would meet in Charleston that had served hard time (many of whom were employed at Fast Company, since they didn't do background checks or give pee tests) were much more humble than Shaun. They didn't walk with their arms flailing about and they certainly didn't have the mouth that Shaun had. Prison had calmed them down, and, on this side of the gate, they were just happy to be alive and in the free world. Of course, their disposition didn't speak to what they might be doing behind the scenes, but nevertheless, they were more compassionate and pleasant to be around. Shaun, on the other hand, was invincible, just like I thought I was at the time, but he had a different way of showing it. It would complicate things between the two of us from time to time when I would get mad if he ordered me to go uptown to pick up his girlfriend after work or whatever, but for the most part we kept things light. Like the time I pulled the truck over to the side of the road after he threw one of his cans out the window.

We had been working together for two weeks, and we were starting to be friends, so I didn't have a problem confronting him about his constant littering. So there we were, sitting in the idle truck on the side of Remount Road one afternoon on our way back to the office.

"What'r you doing?" he asked.

"Look man, check this out. I gotta put my foot down here, bro. If you're gonna be my 'homeboy,' 'my patna,' we're gonna get a few things straight here."

He looked around as if he was on a hidden camera TV show. He wasn't angry, but he was noticeably confused.

"From now on," I continued, "while you're on my truck, there will be no more littering. Every time you throw something out the window, I don't care where we are, I'm gonna pull over and you're going to go pick it up. And while I'm in the business of making demands, you're gonna start buckling your seat belt, too. If you don't like it, well, then it's been nice workin' with ya."

He laughed. He was loving my sudden bossiness. We sat there on the side of the road for a very long ten seconds before he realized that I was not joking around.

"Wait. Are you serious? Are you friggin' kiddin' me? Who the hell are you? My mom?"

Nope. I was his driver. And I wanted to keep it that way. I didn't ask for much. Just two, simple, easy-to-follow demands. And he loved it. He knew that I wasn't an obsessive environmentalist, rather that there were four things that I believed in wholeheartedly: love, hard work, Carolina basketball, and putting your trash in a garbage can.

As he got out of the truck to pick up his can off the ground, murmuring four-letter words my way with a smile on his face the whole time, I knew he was questioning what he had gotten himself into by working with me. Nonetheless, that man stopped littering, and he buckled his seatbelt whenever my truck was moving. It was great. I listened to and respected him, and he did the same in return. We both knew our place. I knew to keep my mouth shut and my ears open when it came to moving furniture, and he knew to bring a bag with him for all of his trash. We learned so much from each other, and we were making good money moving furniture in the process. It was turning out to be a great partnership, Shaun Caldwell and I.

I was hitting a groove and really starting to see the light. I opened a bank account where I deposited my entire paycheck, which ranged from $160 to $250 a week during my first couple of months at Fast Company, depending upon how many hours Shaun and I worked. I also saved all of the money from working with George on Sundays and my tips from the moves as well. Occasionally I slipped by the Goodwill to buy extra shorts for work or Family Dollar to stock up on luxury items like shower slippers and Q-tips and dental floss. But I did my best to conserve my money. Cheap? Frugal? Definitely. But that's how I had to be. Every $5 and $10 I could save might not matter so much for that one day, but it would be so valuable in the long run.

I also continued to donate plasma, since I wasn't afraid of needles, and it was such easy money. I could sit there for an hour and read the paper (which was free in the mornings on the bus!) or a book I had checked out from the library and collect $30 in the meantime.

My eating habits, at least during the day, did suffer quite a bit, though. Lacking the resources to prepare a healthy lunch, I was left snacking throughout the day on what had become my staple diet of peanut butter crackers and canned Vienna Sausage, which was just as appetizing as it sounds. Other days, when I hadn't gone grocery shopping at Family Dollar or I simply needed a break from munching on the same food, I would spring for lunch at McDonald's or Wendy's or any other fast food joint that was convenient for Shaun and me, both in accessibility and price. For $5, I could fill up on the dollar value menu, but it didn't do much to perk up my energy level or balance out my diet. At times, I felt like I could have been starring in Morgan Spurlock's *Super Size Me*. Luckily, Shaun and I had already completed most of our moves by the time we stopped for lunch in the afternoon.

After two weeks working at Fast Company, I took my paycheck stubs down to the Department of Social Services to apply for food stamps. Most of the guys living at the shelter that were unemployed or working cash jobs on the side were getting food stamps. At the time that I was living in the shelter, they were receiving $152 per month. After going through the rigorous application process, which included a thirty-minute meeting with an individually assigned DSS caseworker, I was awarded $80 per month. My caseworker explained that a majority of the consideration for food stamps—similar to the consideration given with Medicare—was given to single mothers. But even with a metabolism that burned food like a furnace, I could make $80 go a long way, especially after I moved out of the shelter.

Life at the shelter remained lively despite the routine: get up, eat, go to work, check to see if my name was highlighted to work the next day, eat, return to the shelter, eat, socialize, shower, argue with some random guy about something ridiculous, and go to bed. My job at Fast Company offered the happy escape that I needed to fraternize with so many different cultures and attitudes. As time dragged on, though, evenings at the shelter started to kill my mood. The longer I lived there, the more I realized what a downer it was to live that lifestyle, and I couldn't wait for the next step in my life, whatever that would be.

Beyond the fact that I was sleeping on a mattress on a floor with more than ninety other men and questioning higher powers as to when I could eat, shower, and wake up in the morning, there were certain things at the shelter that were difficult for me to adjust to. One of those was going to the bathroom. For my first forty-two days in the shelter, I didn't squat on any one of those toilets. I just couldn't do it. I could use the urinal, but other business was taken care of right before I entered the shelter or it was held—often, quite uncomfortably— until the next day. It was the only way. It was so humiliating, to me and probably to many of the other fellas, to sit down on a toilet in an open stall without a door to shield us from everybody that came into the bathroom. The one time that we were supposed to be able to sit back and relax, free from the anxieties and realities of our world, was now a communal event, and the mere thought made me very uncomfortable.

But, I suppose, we adjust. And that's what I was forced to do on day forty-two. Without volunteers to prepare dinner, Robert and a few other shelter inhabitants had whipped up a soon-to-be-infamous concoction of chipped beef with shredded cheese and a side dish of green beans with gravy. It was delicious, no doubt, but the line started forming to use the toilets before everybody had even been served their evening meal. One guy even ate his meal in the bathroom line, knowing that it was going to go right through him. And there I was among them, defaulting on my vow that my cheeks would never touch the stained porcelain lavatories at Crisis Ministries.

We adjust. That's what we do. We seize the opportunities that are given to us, and we adjust to make up for what is kept from us. In some cases, and certainly in the case of the toilets on my forty-second day at the shelter, we don't have a choice. We embrace change or we fight it off. In the end, it is said, change makes us stronger. Even if we deny the change and retreat back to the norm, the experience has helped us to grow and understand what is on that other side, and it has given us the freedom to make more informed decisions in the future.

But I didn't retreat. My first experience using the open-stalled facilities at Crisis Ministries wasn't nearly as bad as I had expected, and it enabled me the freedom to make the choice to come back and use those facilities or not. And I did. Every night. It wasn't as serious of a predicament as I had anticipated, and it definitely wasn't worth the risk of forming ulcers in my stomach if I continued to wait until the next day.

So is it a stretch for me to compare my bathroom habits to life-changing moments? Nope. In fact, on so many levels, change applied to everything I was doing in my everyday life. If there was ever a time for me to embrace change, my time in the shelter was it. I had to make many adjustments if I wanted to get by and eventually get out of the state of poverty that I was in. I was making a complete overhaul in all aspects of my life, from my spending habits to my attitude to the way that I treated my peers. Everywhere. Change. I wasn't changing my personality or who I was. I was changing my outlook on life, and it was affording me the opportunity to really start to appreciate what I had the potential to accomplish in just 365 days.

And that change was so very important, because nobody cared about me. I mean *truly* cared about me. I was on my own, and that was the first tangible realization that I made while I was in the shelter. At first, it was disheartening. When I was young—eleven, twelve, fourteen, eighteen, even twenty-two years old —people were pulling for me. They admired my potential on and off the basketball court, which was enough fuel alone to keep me going. Forget the confidence that I had in myself, I could rely on others for encouragement. At twenty-four, past the "potential stage" and alone in Charleston, it was a completely different situation. I was in the driver's seat, and there were no passengers. I didn't have family or friends to fall back on, and I didn't have people alongside me cheering, really pulling for me. If I succeeded, super. "Good for you, Shep." If not, eh, whatever. Of course, Kazia and the shelter staff were there for me as were my fellow shelter mates, but pass or fail, I was just another person to them. If I succeeded and moved out of the shelter, there was another guy coming in to fill my spot. If I failed and remained at the shelter, there was still another guy coming in with whom I would have to fight for attention. They would do what they could to support me, true, but there were a hundred people that they had to worry about, and there was nothing special about me. Which turned out to be a great situation. Stroking my ego wasn't going to do any good. Handing me $20 might feed me for a few days, but it wasn't going to get me out of the shelter. "Teach a man to fish ..." I was able to learn from the mistakes that Rico and Easy E had made in their lives, and James and Phil Coleman and Kazia offered me guidance, but if I was going to make it out, I was going to make it by my own initiative.

And then, naturally, I started to hit a few bumps in the road. Of course I never expected my odyssey to run smoothly, but I also didn't expect to have so many issues to deal with at once.

At the end of my sixth week in the shelter, I saw Omar for what would turn out to be the last time. I had been worried about him for the duration of my time in the shelter. He would stay out of the shelter for two or three nights and then come to the shelter for the next two or three. I wasn't worried about his safety or ability to cope with life on the streets. Omar Walten could take care of himself. But I could see that he was falling into a funk, that he was losing the spirit that had made him so appealing to me during those first couple of weeks that I knew him.

So during my sixth week, he came into the shelter for his last night, declaring that he was moving to another, more "upscale" shelter down the street, the Pentacalli Mission.

"They charge seventy dollars a week, but it ain't a dump like this place," he declared. "They have beds and closets for each person."

They had a large room in the lobby with sofas and a big screen TV, and most importantly, residents could come and go as they pleased throughout the day. The Pentacalli Mission was more like a youth hostel. To me, the $70 trade-off wasn't worth it, but Omar had had enough of the emotionally draining atmosphere at 573 Meeting Street.

Of course, we didn't mean for it to be the last time we would see each other. But, even after exchanging contact information with the understanding that we would meet with each other whenever possible to make sure that we were still on course to get a place together, I knew that it was probably the last time our paths would cross. We just weren't on the same plane. I tried to kid myself into thinking that I would be living with him at some point in the near future, but it didn't work. I knew the deal. Omar was leaving my life forever, forcing me to steer course in another direction for a living situation. And I wasn't happy about that.

To make matters worse, Shaun was starting to get on my nerves. Big time. He was just so irritable—about everything. Everything on the job was a burden to him, from the furniture to the customers to the hot dogs that he bought at the gas station in the morning. I tried to tell him that those were the same hot dogs that the gas station hadn't sold to him the day before, but he still bought them, and he still complained. After a while, he didn't even want to get along. It was like he wanted to be irritable. Shaun was frustrated with his life, in general, between issues with his girlfriend and the fact that he was paying $40 a night to rent a sleazy hotel room since he wasn't disciplined enough to save enough money to get an apartment. And bringing that stress to work was starting to affect our chemistry. I wasn't sure how much longer Shaun and I could last as a team, but I was sure that I didn't have the power at Fast Company—just yet—to make demands about who my partner would be. If they sent me out with Shaun, they sent me out with Shaun, and there was nothing I could do about it.

Then, bump in the road number three. Four days after Omar moved out of the shelter, I went on a long move with Shaun to Columbia, a couple hours west of Charleston. The move was supposed to be much smaller than it turned out to be—load up a two-bedroom, drive it to Columbia, unload, drive back—but the lady we moved had a heap of stuff, much more than she had mentioned on the phone, and, of course, her apartment in Columbia was on the third floor instead of the first, as the moving sheet had said, so it ended up taking us all day. I dropped Shaun off at his hotel room and pulled into the Fast Company yard at 11:25 PM, exhausted from a day of driving and hauling sofas and mattresses and boxes up the stairs. The No. 10 bus had stopped running, so my options on getting back to the shelter were really limited. I could have called a cab, but the cabs in Charleston take forever to get to you, and it would have cost me at least $15. I could have made the very ambitious walk downtown, but by the time I got back to the shelter, it would have been time for me to hop on the bus to come back to work.

So I grabbed a couple of moving blankets from the back of the truck, and I slept outside. It was a very enlightening experience. Just me and the stars. My body was filthy from the dust and sweat of the move, and I was hungry as hell. And that's when it really hit me: there were people out there sleeping under the stars just like me. For real. Not just for one night, not for some game or some audacious project they were working on. Penniless, hungry, and down and out, they either couldn't get to a shelter or they had chosen the streets instead. But they were out there. I knew all of this before I had lain down on my oh-so-uncomfortable makeshift bed that night, but that's when I really got it. Just as my experience seeing crack-cocaine in person had made everything so real, sleeping outside was opening my eyes as well. I mean, *I* was frustrated and scared and filled with anxiety, and I was only out there for one night! Imagine that. Just for one night, to be sleeping outside without a shower or a meal, I could only imagine what it must be like for the crushed spirits laying their heads down on park benches and under busy overpasses and in sleeping bags in hobo camps throughout the United States. People who would be doing the same thing the next night and the next night and the next. People who had grown up with such ambition, and were now hopeless and discouraged. They had given up, either blind to the aid available at places like Crisis Ministries or shunning it all together. There I was, camping out for a night in the midst of my crazy little adventure, and there they were, wondering what they were going to have to do to get breakfast the next day.

But we trudge on, and that's what I was trying to do. Trudge right along. My finances were coming together nicely, but for whatever reason, I still felt like I was in such a rut, like I wasn't getting anywhere. Omar was gone and Shaun was really starting to try to break me. He knew that my options were limited as far as choosing my own partner, so he knew that he could abuse me. He stopped buckling his seatbelt, and he started throwing his cans out the window again, but I knew better than to get on him. After all, I was just a toothbrush away from a brutal ass-kickin'. He would tell me about his difficult life at home, but I didn't really care to hear it. All of us, in all walks of life, have problems to deal with. *What about my problems, Shaun? Shoot, you don't see me coming to work bitching and complaining and ruining your day.* But I couldn't say anything to him. I was prepared to ride it out until I felt comfortable enough to make the decision to confront Curtis about switching teammates or until I was forced to make that decision.

On Thursday, seven weeks after my induction to Charleston's homeless, I came back to the shelter to find a message waiting for me on the tack board. *Call Curtis from Fast Company. ASAP.*

Terrific.

Curtis only answered the phone when one of his girlfriends was calling, and he rarely called anybody, so the fact that he was calling me at the shelter meant serious business. I didn't have any idea what he could have been calling about, since he knew that I was going to be showing up to work by 7:30 every day. *What could be so important that it couldn't wait until the morning?*

"The money from your move today is missing," he told me when I called. "I got your clipboard and I got the receipt and I got your keys, but there is no cash."

It had been my first cash move since I started working for Fast Company. Most of our customers paid by check or credit card, but occasionally, a smaller move would be paid for with cash. And the cash from my move was missing.

After the move, I had rolled the money up in the receipt, and I had put the money inside the clipboard. We got back to the office after the five o'clock closing time, but Curtis was still there, so I gave him everything. There was an innocent misunderstanding between the two of us where I thought he knew the receipt and the money were inside the clipboard, but he didn't. I left, and he put the clipboard in the pile with the rest of the empty clipboards. The next day, all of the clipboards went out.

So I knew that I didn't have the money, and I knew Curtis wasn't the type of guy who would take the money. Chris, the owner, figured that the money went out the next day with another crew and that their Christmas bonus had come early. I had even been nice enough to gift-wrap the cash in the receipt for them. There was no way for us to find out who had it, and Chris didn't really care. He just wanted his money. Pam, the office manager, split the blame evenly on Curtis (the truck supervisor) and me (the driver in charge of the move) and decided that we would each have to pay $143.50. It was an expensive lesson for both of us, but for me it was even more of a devastating blow, since I was really working my way into a position where I could move out of the shelter soon.

In the end, I didn't read much into the case of the missing loot, since there wasn't much I could do about it anyway. Worrying about it would only add to the stress that I was feeling on so many other fronts in my life, so I went to the bank, withdrew the money, and paid Pam the $143.50.

Interestingly enough, the one person that was keeping my spirits up was the bus driver in the morning. No joke. Every morning when I boarded the bus, there he was with a huge smile and a "Good Morning!" At 6:45 AM. And the bus ride would always be filled with funny comments as he conversed with regular customers or picked on somebody for his or her choice of attire or not giving their seat up for a lady. I was excited just to have the free copy of *The Post and Courier*, but he made the trip even more worth the inexpensive fare.

One short week and I had experienced enough drama and turmoil to last my entire year. Mentally, I had been prepared to deal with whatever came my way, but that didn't erase the fact that I had been so high on life seven days before, and then, just like that, I was left picking up the pieces, wondering if I was ever going to get out of the shelter.

But I knew that in the pendulum of life, the momentum would have to swing in my direction eventually. And my pendulum was nearing its negative peak and preparing to swing back my way.

ELEVEN

MOVIN' ON UP

❦

O r so I thought.

It was my first move downtown, and my first experience learning that moving downtown was kind of like an arranged marriage—you hope for the best, you never really know what you're going to get until you get there, and then, one way or another, you're totally overwhelmed.

Or, you break your toe.

I was on the move with a random guy, Phillipe, since Shaun had some other important business to deal with. According to the sheet, the move would be a two-bedroom, one living room, one dining room, and one home office. Usually, that would have been a three-man move, but tough guys Phillipe and I told Curtis and Pam that since they were short on movers for the day, we could handle it ourselves.

Huge mistake. After about three hours and my sixth trip down the stairs carrying toiletries and hanging clothes, I started to slow down—a first in my moving career. I was so pissed off. It was one of those rare moves where the customer was grossly unprepared. That lady hadn't packed anything. Not a single thing. Some in-town moves can be way different from moves that go across state lines, and I was coming to that brutal realization. "Hell, we're only going twelve minutes away, honey. We don't need any boxes."

Generally, I wouldn't have minded since we were getting paid by the hour and the less prepared the customer was, the more hours we received. But that move was an exception to the rule. Mentally, if not physically, I thought I was actually starting to become a real mover—a power mover—and I didn't have time to worry about petty stuff, like packing the nooks and crannies of a house. Little items or little pieces of furniture were a burden to me. "Here, man, carry this nightstand. I'm gonna grab this dresser." My head had begun to swell in my short stint at Fast Company, which is pretty funny, since I really wasn't even that proficient a mover.

So, anyway, there I was, doing my best to stay focused, thinking of what kind of system I could rig up so that we could just toss that lady's crap down the stairs to make things go quicker. She was on the phone making real estate deals, and she didn't seem to care at all about the laborious job to which she had sentenced us. In fact, she was totally oblivious to it. One time when I was passing by her, she told the person on the other end of her phone conversation to hold on, and she asked me, "Hey, Adam, do you know how long you guys are gonna be, because I have an important meeting to get to?"

"Well ma'am, if you hold on just one second, let me load this desk lamp and these baking sheets onto the truck, and I'll take a walk through and see what kind of estimate I can make."

But I didn't make an estimate. I couldn't. That move was just too unpredictable, and I tried to explain that to her. "There's just no tellin', ma'am." She walked away in a huff, and so did I.

But in the process of my huff, I bumped into some lawn chairs leaning up against the wall, which knocked over a hundred-pound steel plate that was also resting on the wall. And I couldn't move my size fourteens out of the way quick enough. The steel plate fell directly on my right big toe, crushing it.

I'm not sure which was more impressive: the flamboyant dance that I did immediately afterward as I jumped around the room in pain or how colorful my toe had turned when I removed my shoe and sock at the end of the move.

That's right, at the end of the move. Man, I wish I hadn't finished that move, but there really wasn't much of a choice. I could have called for reinforcements, but that would have been so much of a hassle and, in the process, I would have been whisked to the wayside as just another regular mover.

Besides, when I came downstairs to tell Phillipe that I thought I had broken my toe, he just said, "Yeah, man, that sucks. Owwie. My toe hurts, too. Hey can you hand me that chair right there?"

So I hobbled around for the rest of the day, each step more painful than the last. I would have thought that I would eventually become desensitized to the pain, but that was not the case at all. It kept hurting, throbbing. We finished the move at 7:30 that evening, and Phillipe dropped me off at the hospital on his way back to the shop. I sat in the waiting room for three hours showing off my toe to the kids running around, and then the doctors took X-rays to determine that I had, in fact, broken my big toe. The doctor prescribed antibiotics and pain medication and explained that I would have to keep the toe elevated for five days. It was going to cost Fast Company $825 just for that feeble advice alone, forget the follow-up visits.

I had been so ready to move out of the shelter, to "move on up," but instead I was destined to be stuck in there until I was back on my feet. I was banking all of my money (more than $1,500, in fact), so I felt I had a comfortable security net in the event that I was faced with any kind of hardship, like losing my job. I had been working with George every Sunday and he mentioned that Mickey, his close friend who I had met briefly when I buried his dead dog along with my regular Sunday chores, had a room in his house downtown that he would rent me for $100 a week. "The room is a bit less than exciting, but it's a pretty nice house, and you'll have the run of the kitchen," he said. I was sold. I figured that I could live there for a couple of months while I looked for something more permanent. The monthly rent would be about the same, if not just a few bucks more expensive, than staying in the neighborhood by the shelter, so I reasoned that it was the best all-around deal that I was going to find.

But my financial stability was only one of the reasons that I was ready to get out of the shelter. As much as I knew I was going to miss the shelter—the camaraderie, the excitement, the bizarre conversations, and the food—it was such a drag to have to come back to the shelter to be around guys that didn't share my same motivation. Several of them had done their part in telling me the direction I needed to be headed, and the time had come for me to hit the road.

On Friday, September 22, my sixtieth day at the shelter, I had given Harold, the front desk worker, my two-day warning.

"Two days? Super. Thanks for the notice, Shep." He picked up a pen and pretended to write. "Shepard ... two days ... got it. You're all set. Hopefully we can get somebody in here to fill your spot."

As a practical matter, he didn't care if I stayed for two more days or two hundred, but we had become friends over the previous couple of months, so I figured he'd like to know what I was up to.

"You're gonna do a'ight, Shep," he said. "Just stay out of trouble, and you're gonna do a'ight."

I was planning on it. Out of trouble and on course. That's where I was, and in two more days I would have been living in Mickey's attic-room downtown, free to come and go as I pleased and free to finally sleep without a chorus of snorers in the background.

But then I got hurt. Which was natural and expected, I suppose. Why should anything go as planned? And just like that, my daily routine had shifted from exciting to mundane. I would wake up in the morning, eat breakfast with everybody else, and then go back to bed until lunch. After lunch, I would go back to bed until dinner. After dinner, I would go back to bed until breakfast the next day. For five days straight. I would hold off going to the bathroom as long as possible since my foot throbbed painfully every time I brought it down from its elevation. I ran out of reading material early on day two, so I spent the remaining time just lying there, looking at the ceiling with my foot elevated on top of my gym bag. It was hell on Earth, a character builder like none other. I would have rather been outside doing something, anything, than cooped up in that place for five days straight. The only good thing about my injury was that I got to hear more war stories about guys who had been injured on the job: accidents at the paper mill, falls from second floors, and missing fingers. One guy showed me a huge scar above his knee that spanned half of the circumference of his thigh where he had almost cut his leg clean off with a chainsaw. I looked at my toe, and then I looked at his leg. And then I looked back at my toe. "Sissy," I told him, pointing to my injury. "I bet your leg didn't turn that color, did it?"

And each war story that I heard would end with the narrator exclaiming, "Wait, were you wearing steel-toed boots? Cuz you shoulda been wearin' steel-toed boots. I'da been wearin' steel-toed boots."

Following the doctor's orders was the easiest part of my injury since I wanted to be out of there as soon as possible. I took my medication and stayed on bed rest for those five days. Fortunately, Fast Company was able to survive those days without me, and when I went back five days after the injury, boss lady Pam was very accommodating about my injury. "I've got plenty for you to do," she said. The doctor had informed me that I still wasn't going to be allowed to move furniture for two to three weeks after my release from bed rest, so Pam put me to work around the office for twenty-five to thirty hours per week. She had me answering phones, filing paperwork, and performing other paltry office duties, but I didn't hate it.

In hindsight, as I recollect my broken toe experience, I realize how fortunate I had been.

What if this had happened to one of my buddies who had been washing dishes and had no money saved up at all? What if his boss wasn't as tolerant? His injury would be covered by insurance, sure, but what would happen if he were let go?

What if I had broken my leg instead of a toe and I was sent home for two months instead of two weeks?

What if that experience happened to a working mom, and time off with a meager workers' compensation check sunk her financially or she was unable to get her kids to and from daycare?

I suppose that these type of "what if" questions lead to even more questions than answers, and that the chain has to be broken off at some point. It happened, I hit a roadblock. OK, now what do I do? I could complain about my situation and feel sorry for myself or I could get back on the horse. If nothing else, I was discovering that life just simply isn't fair, but the difference emerges among the people that accept that ideal, embrace it even, and bask in the unsung glory of knowing that each obstacle overcome along the way only adds to the satisfaction in the end. Nothing great, after all, was ever accomplished by anyone sulking in his or her misery.

Office work at Fast Company provided a short enough release for me to take a recess from heavy lifting, but a long enough break for me to be rejuvenated and ready to get back to work.

And I was excited to get back out in the field. Even better yet, without Shaun. While I was laid up in the office, Pam received an anonymous letter from a customer complaining about Shaun's drinking on the job. The customer wrote that Shaun's antics were unprofessional and embarrassing for the company and that some sort of action should be taken. Pam had evidently had enough of Shaun's mouth around the office anyway, and receiving a letter like that warranted his immediate dismissal from the company. After nearly two months, my partnership with Shaun came to an end. Some guys would miss him and others didn't think twice about his dismissal. But I suppose that's how it is in the moving business and so many other blue-collar service industries where many guys are expendable. It was a revolving door. One guy out, another guy in. Before I returned to moving furniture, though, I moved out of the shelter. And I wasn't the only one. Omar was gone. James was getting out soon, and so, at least according to his own intentions, was Larry. Even Easy E and Rico had left on Sunday night, bound for a six-month drug rehab program in Fort Lauderdale, Florida, sponsored by Battalion Baptist Church.

There were so many personalities in the shelter, and I had met them all. The good guys and the bad guys. The aggressively angry and the eerily mellow. The drunk and the sober. The lazy and the energetic. Those who felt blessed by the Lord and those who cursed him for their plight. Those who would give you their last bar of soap and those who would try to steal it from you. I had feasted and showered and laid my head next to them all.

I packed my bags on a Monday night, my birthday. It was my most memorable birthday ever. Somebody found a cupcake and a candle in the kitchen and they lit it and wished me a happy birthday. No singing. No balloons. No funny hats or party favors. Just plenty of well wishes. It was an emotional moment for me. I could only hope, as I packed my belongings to move out the next day, that the guys in there understood what an impact they had made on my life. I knew it wouldn't be easy to leave the familiar atmosphere of the shelter, going into a situation where I would once again be alone and among the unknown, but I couldn't help but appreciate the spirit that I was taking with me. Several guys in the shelter had really aggravated me with their lethargic behavior, but other guys had inspired me to sail onward. And that was the legacy that I was carrying with me as I moved downtown to Mickey's attic-turned-bedroom.

And it was good that I was taking a solid morale with me down there, because the accommodations were almost as bad as the shelter.

I had my own room, which was great, but that room was a fourteen-by-fourteen cell with ceilings that were shorter than I was. I had to bend down to walk about the room, bumping my head at least once every couple of days. The previous habitant, from several years before, had left a futon mattress on the floor, so at least I had a place to lay my sleeping bag. It was cleaner, to a certain extent, than the shelter, but the bathroom that Mickey had added upstairs at some point over the years hadn't been cleaned in quite some time. So I cleaned it and dusted and mopped the floor in my room, and I prepared to call it home for two months. Mickey's four-story house was just like each of the other unique, elegant houses squashed together throughout the bottom of the peninsula that had been standing since before the Civil War. Though old and rickety, the first three floors were lavish and very homey, complete with elegant furnishings and splendid artwork. Even though I was confined to either the kitchen or my hole in the wall on the fourth floor, I was grateful to have some place to stay that I could consider my own, and I was now even more compelled to continue my steady progression upward. Avoiding complacency, I was cruising through my project quicker than I had imagined I would.

On Wednesday morning, I woke up and left the house at 6:00 AM so that I could make the thirty-minute walk to the bus stop. My toe was still tender, but I was more than ready to get back to moving. The doctors told me that the tenderness would go away eventually as the remaining cracked bones in my toe filled in. In five or six more weeks, I would have full mobility. They could tell that I was going to lose my toenail eventually, but I wasn't worried about that. It had been overgrown anyway.

I got to the shop that Wednesday morning at 7:15, happy to be back in uniform and ready to tackle whatever kind of move they wanted to throw at me. At that point, I didn't really care who they stuck me with or where they sent me.

And that's when I met him.

For everything that was said about him, Derrick Hale didn't look like anything special to me. Considering all of the hype I had heard about what a sensational mover he was, I was expecting a seven-foot tall monster with a good three hundred pounds of muscle. He wasn't this stoic character, though, like the meatheads you see in movies—without a thought, just a lot of power. Nope. Quite the opposite, actually. Five foot eight, 160, normal build. He was, well, normal looking, just like any other guy that I had seen running around Charleston.

But the fact was that there was nothing normal about Derrick Hale. After less than three years on the job, he had catapulted himself to the top of the list as *the* guy that everyone wanted to work with. He was legendary, the best, irrefutably, and nobody, not a single person that I had encountered at Fast Company, had said anything different. JB was stronger, DeWayne "Too Tall" McGovern was faster on his feet, and Old Man Jimmy could pack the truck better. But as far as the total package—strength, quickness, stamina, and knowledge—Derrick Hale was far and away ahead of the rest. Which made it even more of an enigma that I had been assigned to work with him on my first Wednesday back on the job.

I figured I would always be a small timer, working one- and two-bedroom moves throughout the duration of my time at Fast Company. Which was fine with me. I was doing well, and I was certainly on course to reach my goals in my specified time frame. But everything changed on that Wednesday, my first day back on the trucks in three weeks. Derrick's driver, too, had quit ("That weak cat couldn't lift a four-drawer filing cabinet," was the ultimate put down, the humor being that Hercules himself couldn't lift a four-drawer filing cabinet), and we were more or less thrown together at the last minute for the move that day—a three-bedroom move in Park West, Mount Pleasant's largest neighborhood. By chance or mistake, he was assigned to work with me. As much as I would love to say that Derrick had heard that I was starting to learn the trade pretty quickly and that I was a good listener and that I was a good catch as a driver, that wasn't the case at all. He didn't have a clue who I was. Even though I clearly stood out with my floppy hair and tall, gangly frame, he still hadn't paid any attention to me during my initial eight weeks as a mover. There was a pecking order at Fast Company, which was determined by our performance on the job, and after eight weeks on the job, I was still a bottom feeder.

So while I was expecting Mr. Hard-ass, he, again, defied my rumored images of him by treating me like we were long-lost buddies who had been separated for years and were finally reuniting. We talked about my life, where I was from, what I did for fun, and how my skinny legs and abnormally large shoes made me look like Ronald McDonald. We talked the whole way to the job. It was unbelievable. I was on edge the whole time. I learned about him, and he learned about me. There I was, sitting alongside the greatest mover at Fast Company, and I felt like I belonged. It was a remarkable feeling.

Once we got to the job, though, we buckled down. Which is not to say that we didn't joke and socialize throughout the day, but things were certainly more serious when we were on the job. We had work to do, and all three of us did it. (Mike, another renowned mover at Fast Company, was out there with us too, but I was invisible to him). We wrapped the furniture, carried it out, loaded it on the truck, and drove to the unload. Our process was fluid, without hesitation. Every room was full, so it was a large move, but we knocked it out in six hours.

"I like you, Adam," Derrick had said on the way to the unload, surprisingly early in our partnership. "Don't take it to heart, cuz I like everybody, but you're a'ight with me."

Derrick was more than "a'ight" with me. Working with him was so different than my experience with Shaun. Sure, Derrick was a marvel to watch, carrying a dryer or a recliner or three boxes of books onto the truck at once, packing them in, and then going back for more. And he would literally jog from the truck back into the house to pick up another piece. His style of moving was very remarkable, no doubt, but what struck me most about him was his modesty. Shaun walked and talked like he was something pretty special; Derrick didn't. He was the best, and he knew he was the best, but he also knew that his work spoke for itself. He didn't stop to take long breaks, and he surely didn't slow down after he started. He was friendly to the customer, but he didn't waste time with idle chitchat as other guys that I had worked with would do.

In fact, he and I didn't talk much on the job on that day. He didn't boss me around, and he didn't explicitly teach me anything. Nothing. I'm not sure if he was sizing me up to see how I worked or if he figured he wouldn't be working with me again anyway, so why should he bother, but either way, I was anxious all day long. I couldn't tell if my technique was good or bad, but as the day wore on and the more I saw him working, the less confidence I had in my own feeble moving abilities. At that point, I was more qualified than when I had started at Fast Company, but I was starting to doubt the tactics that Shaun had taught me. Derrick was carrying two pieces to my one, which, even considering both his dominance and my bum toe, was still ridiculous. I couldn't hang with him, but I still found comfort in the fact that nobody else could either.

Perhaps all of this may seem like it couldn't have really been that serious, like I'm being dramatic in my description of Derrick. After all, who the hell were we? We were movers! We were nobodies! Most of us had dropped out or barely graduated from high school and we were destined to be blue-collar workers for the rest of our days. But that's just it! That's what was so special about Derrick and several of the other guys that I met at Fast Company and in other areas of Charleston. Nobodies, like Derrick and Mike, were difference makers, legends in their own world. They were providing a service that was so very necessary and they were very good at what they were doing. There was a huge contrast, in attitude and otherwise, that separated guys like Derrick (who took their job seriously, wanted to excel, and wanted to be proud of what they had accomplished) from the guys who you could tell were coming to work just to make a few bucks to pay their rent. Moving furniture was so much more than that to guys like Derrick and Mike. They were professionals, seasoned veterans who had made sacrifices to put themselves in a position to do things that no one else could do. They were average guys performing above average feats.

But, then again, so were many other people I met along my trip in Charleston and in my life in general. It's like in the movie *Castaway* where Tom Hanks's character returns from being on the island for five years and is in shock at the massive food platters at a party, a lighter, the pocket knife—ordinary things. I was in shock.

And that's how I felt about the bus driver, too.

I decided that Friday would be the last day of riding the bus, as I planned to car hunt over the weekend. I didn't know the bus driver on a personal level, nor did I think I would have cared so much about his services, but I did. He was like many other people in my life, but this time I decided to acknowledge him. So I wrote him a note:

Dear Mr. Bus Driver, whose name I don't know and whose path I will never cross again in my life:

It's incredible how insignificantly significant guys like you and I are. It's interesting how in the grand scheme of life, we have the power to wake up and make a difference in the world. Or not. You and me: a regular old bus driver and a regular old mover.

Every day, Monday through Friday, I ride your bus, and every day, Monday through Friday, you get my day started off right. You greet every rider with a smile and a "Good morning" and you proceed to brighten everybody's day with common conversation or witty comments. It doesn't matter who gets on your bus or how long they ride, when they hop off your bus, with a regenerated hop in their step, their demeanor has inevitably changed for the better.

You do that. You! Otherwise irrelevant and unimportant in this crazy, self-indulgent world of ours, you find some way to be selfless. It isn't fake and there surely aren't any ulterior motives behind your actions. After all, you aren't going to benefit financially by being a great guy. You aren't going to get tips from the clientele that ride your bus. As a matter of fact, you're going to get your same paycheck regardless of what kind of attitude you bring to work.

But are you even really that special? I mean, you don't do my taxes, you can't represent me in the courtroom, and you can't operate on me if I tear ligaments in my knee. You're not a big shot, and you don't bring home a six-figure salary. You're just, well, a normal, run-of-the-mill kind of guy.

Except that you're not normal. Which is the reason I'm writing to you.

I'm writing this note to you because I've ridden other buses, and I've had other bus drivers. Some are cordial and some are not. Some smile and some don't. Some have an extra quarter lying around if we're short on fare and others are penny-pinchers. Some can't wait for the workday to end, while others, like you, represent what is naturally good about our society today.

We are so very necessary, guys like you and I. After all, without us, who is going to drive buses or move furniture? Who is going to fix cars or serve breakfast to those doctors and lawyers and accountants?

The crazy thing is that there are millions of people like you around our country! Just as there are millions of people with poor attitudes who wake up with selfish intentions, there are people like you, who wake up with the purpose of making a difference in somebody's day. They're everywhere. Bankers, construction workers, retail employees, landscapers, and roofers; doctors' assistants, dental hygienists, restaurant managers, and used car salesmen. Well, bad example, but you get the idea. The simple fact is that some people will go through their lives virtually unnoticed, while others, like you, will be remembered.

And I would just like to say "Thank you." Thank you for making a difference in my life, however small you think that difference may be.

Today is my last day riding your bus. Chances are, I will never see you again, but at the same time, I want you to know that I will never forget you.

Cheers,
Adam Shepard

As I handed him the letter and exited the bus on that Friday morning, I really felt good about what I had written. My letter to the bus driver was applicable to so many people in so many walks of life. There are many reasons that America is the greatest country in the world, and guys like the bus driver represented a great deal of that reality. He—just like everybody else—had a right to a place in our society. He belonged. I could have made copies of that letter and started handing them out to people that had made a difference in my life in my two months in Charleston; people that had made a difference in my life since I had had the capacity to retain memory; people who had really shaped me to be the person that I had become; people who had made a difference maybe just once; and people that had been major factors in my growth: family, friends, bosses, coaches, and teachers. Average people performing above average feats.

I told Pam and Curtis that I would need Saturday off so that I could go car hunting. I had stocked up on cereal, milk, and orange juice, and

I had prepaid a month's rent to Mickey, which left me with just shy of $1,750 in the bank. I wasn't sure what kind of car I would be looking for, but I knew the price: $1,000. Spending a grand of my money on a car would leave me with enough money in the bank for a couple of months of insurance and about $400 in the event that something went wrong with my new automobile.

If there was one thing that Max at *Max's Made-Over Motors* had going for him, it was that I wasn't going to be shopping around. It wasn't that I didn't have the time or the patience to hunt for a good deal, rather I figured that I was taking a gamble by buying a car for $1,000 anyway, so there wasn't much of a difference between the lemons I was going to get at *Max's* versus the lemons I would get anywhere else.

I didn't know much about the operation of automobiles either. After a test drive, I planned to take any prospective buy to a transmission specialist who could give me a diagnostic test for $50 and determine if the transmission was in good condition. The only repairs that would totally break my bank account involved the transmission. The emergency money that I had set aside could cover a busted water pump or a new timing belt, but if the transmission went, I would probably have to sack it and buy another car.

Max wasn't around, but Jimmy Jr. (Max's son, he told me), took me around the lot of about twenty or so cars to help me find one to take for a test drive. I settled on a silver pickup truck with a $900 price tag on the windshield. I hopped in and told Jimmy Jr. that I was going to take it to "my transmission guy" and that I would be right back.

"Hold up, are you kiddin'?" he asked, a funny, contemplative look plastered on his face. "You think you're just gonna drive that truck off the lot?"

I was clearly unfamiliar with the system of taking cars for a test drive, and Jimmy Jr. was really intrigued that I thought I was simply going to drive away in his pickup truck. He looked at me for a second, confused almost to the point of laughter. Then, he laughed.

"You can't be serious. Where you takin' it, did you say?"

"To my transmission guy, up there at Willis Transmission Specialists."

"I can't believe I'm doing this. My pappy is gonna kill me."

Because he knew that I was serious about buying a car, he let me take it, but I wasn't gone long. I didn't drive a half a mile away from the lot before I realized why the truck was priced at $900. Whenever I shifted from first to second or second to third, the car would hesitate for a moment and then kick into gear. I didn't know what kind of problem that was, but I knew that I would at least like to own the car for a little while before it had a problem like that. So I returned to the shop for my second choice, a beautiful 1988 GMC Sierra S-15 pickup truck. Black, without a scratch on its exterior.

So that was the one I ended up taking to the transmission guy up the street from the used car dealership on Rivers Avenue. It took him fifteen minutes to hook it up to the computer, return no codes, and determine that the transmission was in good shape. Which was all I needed to hear. It was driving fine, and besides a host of aesthetic problems on the inside (passenger side window stuck in the "down" position, driver side window stuck in the "up" position, sun visors missing, leather interior torn to shreds, dirty floor mats, no radio, just to start the list), I wanted it. I didn't care that it would repel the ladies or that it could only seat about a person and a half comfortably. That baby got eighteen miles to the gallon and had a reputation for running forever.

But I didn't tell any of that to Jimmy Jr. I got back to the dealership and put on my serious, negotiating face.

"Well?" he asked. "What'd them boys say?"

"Shoot, man. They said it was a'ight. They wouldn't buy it, but I might still be interested." If nothing else, I had just dropped $50 for the diagnostic test, so I wanted to see what kind of deal we could work out.

The S-15 didn't have a price tag on it, but I assumed that it would be right around the same price as the first pickup truck I had taken for a test run. In any event, those prices are just a starting line for us consumers to work down from anyway.

"How much are you askin' for that guy, anyway?" My disposition was so nonchalant.

"That'n there, we're askin' fifteen hundred."

Ha! I thought, before I realized he was serious. How was I ever going to work my way down to a grand from that?

"Man, that is a little high for me," I said, straightening my disposition. "There are so many things wrong with it on the inside. Y'know, windows and the radio missing and all. I think I can spare about seven-fifty."

Wow. Get a load of that aggressiveness, huh? Using the windows and radio as leverage, I had cut the price in half. But my face didn't show it. If we were playing poker and I was holding a straight flush, he wouldn't have known.

"Seven hundred and fifty *dollars*?" He looked at me with the same look as he had when I started taking the first pickup off the lot. He laughed at me again. He really did think I was kidding. I didn't mean to but he was clearly insulted, as in, "Get the hell outta my face before I sic the dogs on yer ass."

But I persisted. "Yeah. I mean, is that too low?"

"Too low? Boy, you're at the wrong place to try to make deals like that."

"Well, why don't you just give Mighty Max a call and see what he says." *Mighty Max?* Ha. It was going to be a long weekend for me and my wise-guy attitude.

"I'm gonna call 'im. And I'm gonna give 'im yer offer, but he prolly gonna hang up on me."

But Max, good ol' Mighty Max, didn't hang up. We negotiated back and forth through his son Jimmy Jr. and after a lot of huffing and puffing and shrugging and hard thinking on both sides, we settled on $1,000.

In hindsight, though, I wondered if Jimmy Jr. was even on the phone with his dad or if there even was a Max at the helm of that dealership. I wondered what was really wrong with that truck that he was letting it go for $500 below his asking price. Chances are I had been played just as bad as I thought I was playing them. Probably worse.

But none of that mattered. We'd made the deal, and both sides were happy even though we both kept shaking our heads, swearing we were giving away the deal of a lifetime. I got my truck for the price I had set out to spend, and Jimmy Jr. unloaded another automobile off his lot. We did the paperwork, and I drove off in my new ride, a huge stride in the grand scheme of what I had set out to accomplish.

I hadn't worked with Derrick on Thursday or Friday, and by the weekend I had discounted the idea that I would ever get to work with him again.

But that turned out not to be the case. I was assigned to work with Mike and him again on Monday. And Tuesday. And Wednesday. On Thursday, Derrick told me that he thought it would be a great idea if we formed a crew. Forget a poker face; I couldn't hold back my enthusiasm. I acted as if I had just been given a promotion and I was giving my acceptance speech. "Oh, man. That's great. I promise I won't let you down." I'm pretty sure I hugged him. It wasn't embarrassing, though. By that fourth day working together, Derrick and I were on the same wavelength. Even though I was the driver and theoretically the head of the crew, we both knew who the boss was, and he knew that I would pretty much do anything he asked. We had hit it off from the beginning, and it was looking like ours was going to be a long-lasting relationship.

Working with Derrick was like starting over again at Fast Company, except more challenging. I had to unlearn everything that Shaun had taught me (which wasn't necessarily wrong, just less efficient), and then learn the way Derrick did things. His system. Fortunately,

Derrick was very patient with me, recognizing that I really wanted to learn his profession, and that no matter how bad I was and how many mistakes I made, I would work hard in the process. Identifying the limits of my capabilities early on, he found ways to take full advantage of my strengths. He could tell that I wasn't particularly strong ("Man, that's all you got?" he would say), but he also knew that I had the stamina of a Kenyan in the Boston Marathon. I could work all day long without stopping. For the first month or so, he and Mike would take care of the pieces that were terribly heavy, but as time passed, I began to get stronger.

Getting to know Derrick was way different than getting to know Omar. I can tell now that my relationship with Omar was doomed from the beginning. It had been too good to be true. Too convenient, too soon. I had gone looking for an Omar, and when I found him, I became so attached that I wouldn't let go until I had to. Omar, as it turned out, couldn't have cared less either way.

But my relationship with Derrick was different. It was very real. Neither one of us needed each other and we certainly hadn't gone looking for each other. Indeed, I was content on small moves with whomever they stuck me with, and Derrick was fully capable of doing most of the moves by himself. But then we met and worked together, and everything changed. The chemistry between us—which, I discovered, was so utterly important in the moving business—was established from the beginning. He knew that I was going to work hard and keep my mouth shut, and I knew that he was going to show me how it was really supposed to be done, in turn exploiting my full potential as a professional mover.

With Derrick on my team, or vice versa, there was no more time for child's play. Just as I was getting used to cruising down the highway in truck No. 2, I was moved to truck No. 4—still a stick shift, but bigger, with a 26' storage van. Ninety percent of our moves were three bedrooms or better with an occasional two bedroom thrown in the mix when Mike had to take a day off. My moving experience was jumping to the next level. No more twenty to twenty-five hour workweeks. All of our moves lasted at least six hours, with quite a few going eight hours or longer. It made for an exhausting day, no doubt, but that is what I had asked for when I came to Charleston—the full blue-collar experience. And there was no question I was getting it.

TWELVE

WORKERS' CONSTERNATION

❧

Bigger moves meant more hours and bigger tips. I was cashing in.
I was glad that Phil Coleman had deterred me away from the car
wash. I still would have been doing well there, with an hourly wage
plus tips, but I would have been doing the same thing day in and
day out: Wax on, wax off, fifty times a day, all week long. Of course,
I would have done it, and I would have done it with a smile on my
face, but I wouldn't have had the same experience that I had moving
furniture.

Working as a mover was great. It offered me the escape from
reality that I needed. Even though moving was probably the most
stressful job I could have chosen, it was fun to be out and about
doing a different job every day. Every day was exclusive of the next.
Different moves, different personalities.

Some of our moves were downtown, in the heart of Charleston;
others were in country towns like Eutawville or Pinopolis where it
might take residents twenty minutes to ride into town just for gas
and groceries.

Some customers were bright and cheery; some were all business.

Some were completely unorganized, while others had every box and each piece of furniture coded by number or color corresponding to where it was supposed to be placed at their new house.

Some bought us lunch and offered us beverages throughout the day; others wouldn't have cared if we passed out from dehydration on their front lawn.

Some were snobbish; others were modest.

And I loved meeting new people. For most of the day, I wasn't "Adam Shepard, the loner" or "Adam Shepard, the guy who recently moved out of the homeless shelter." I was "Adam Shepard, Mover Extraordinaire." My crew and I would sweat and socialize at the same time, all the while making one-day friends in the process. After all, our customers—every one of our customers—were more privileged than we were. While many of the guys at Fast Company lived pretty exciting lives, our experiences were much different from those of the people that we moved. They didn't have to break the bank for weekend trips to Myrtle Beach or to go out to dinner at elegant restaurants downtown. They traveled to Europe and Australia and Southeast Asia. They had sailed to the Bahamas or made long treks by bicycle or hiked the Appalachian Trail. And their children would go to prestigious universities, schools like Clemson or Winthrop or somewhere out of state.

Once in a while, at the hands of ignorance rather than disrespect, our customers would show their superiority. One day early in my moving career, I had a conversation with a customer whose son had worked as a mover on weekends for a while.

"Said it was the hardest work he ever did," she said.

"Well, he wasn't lying," I replied. "What does he do now?"

"Oh, his back started bothering him. He's got a real job now."

But, more often than not, lines of respect went both ways. Just as we were in awe (and a wee bit envious) of the houses that we moved, many of our customers admired the occupation that we had chosen to make our living. And it was great to be appreciated. Just as there was absolutely no prestige in any of the jobs that I had performed in my first couple of weeks in Charleston, moving was different. People were impressed to see us performing tasks that they couldn't or wouldn't do. And it wasn't just the children watching our every move with looks of reverence, exclaiming, "Wow, look at him lift that all by himself, Daddy." More often than not, the customers themselves would end up looking at *me* sometime throughout the day, saying, "Wow, look at Derrick carrying that all by himself. Shouldn't somebody grab the other end?" Recliners, huge coffee tables, solid oak headboards, bookshelves—it was mind boggling the things that guy could lift.

And Trinitrons. Ugh, Trinitrons. Even in the wake of the popularity of featherweight plasma home theater systems, Sony's grossly overweight Trinitron televisions were maintaining their market share. Trinitrons were our worst nightmare, infamous for their awkwardly heavy design. I would have rather wrestled with any fifty-two-inch projection TV than dealt with a twenty-six-inch Trinitron. They were that heavy, and so unnecessary. The manufacturing company must use the Trinitron as an outlet to dispose of all of the unused parts at the manufacturing plant. "Say, uh, Marshall, we won't be needing any of these iron scraps. Just melt them down and toss them in one of those Trinitrons." I can't tell you exactly how much those things weigh, but I can tell you that it was a rough way to start the day. We would arrive at a house and do a walk-through with the customer to see what exactly we would be moving—sofas, tables, desks, bookshelves, refrigerators, dressers, armoires. No problem. The weight was more evenly distributed on those pieces and with the assistance of special dollies, we could two-man them out the door. But then we would spot a Trinitron, and a collective sigh would pass over the room. One of us would throw out some sarcastic wise-crack to try to ease the discomfort, but there was no escaping the fact that somebody—two somebodies if Derrick wasn't in "He-Man Mode"—was going to have to carry that beast out the door.

But Derrick, in all of his glory, never made me look bad. If anything, he made me shine. My awkwardness made it clear to all of our customers who was the veteran and who was the rookie on our team, but at the same time, we complemented each other nicely. With the dollies and the efficiency of the furniture wrapping system, we could each clear a room by ourselves. Derrick would wrap and clear one room, while I was wrapping and clearing another room, while Mike was wrapping and clearing another room. If one of us needed a hand with something, we would call for assistance, and then everybody would get back to working on his room. Our nearly flawless efficiency was putting a smile on the customers' faces, and, as I said, a happy customer meant bigger tips.

It was good that I was putting those extra dollars in my pocket. In addition to putting a good amount of it in the bank, I was able to eat, purchase car insurance ($350 when I prepaid for a year), pay Mickey the weekly rent, and keep my truck fueled.

And pay speeding fines.

With nine speeding tickets already to my credit (which is particularly impressive since I didn't even own a car for four years in college), there was one main reason that I bought a pickup truck: I wasn't going to get pulled over. I mean, really, how many times do you see a pickup truck on the side of the road with blue lights flashing behind it? Pretty much never, unless there's a gun rack in the window and Billy Ray is wanted on suspicion of some drug charge. But that was me on the side of Rivers Avenue on the last Sunday morning in October, just two weeks after I had driven my truck off of Max's lot. It had started to drizzle, and since rolling up the window was a two-hand operation, I simply lost track of how fast I was going.

At first, I was kind of happy that my truck was even capable of speeding. "Atta boy!" But then the officer handed me the $128 speeding ticket—no warning, nothing—and things got a little more serious. I tried to tell him that it would never happen again, and yadda, yadda, yadda—sob stories that he had heard a thousand times—but it was too late. I would join him in court in mid-November.

When I got to court, I petitioned the judge to let me do community service in lieu of paying such a hefty fine, but he wasn't interested in negotiations. I paid the fine and determined that I would simply have to slow down.

Which wasn't hard to do, since, aside from work, I didn't have anywhere to be. With Omar gone and my only other friend Derrick married, my social life was maintaining its status on suicide watch throughout the duration of my stay at Mickey's house downtown. But that wasn't necessarily a bad thing, since I was staying focused. I wasn't even upset with the fact that my life had become so mechanical, since I knew that once I was living in a more permanent setting, I would have plenty of opportunities to hang out and stay out late. Besides, in those early days on Derrick's crew, I was usually so beat after a full day of work that I didn't have the desire to go out. Generally speaking, after a move, I would go home, write in my journal, read, eat, and go to bed. I did, however, find myself missing the companionship from my days at the shelter.

Chris, the owner of Fast Company, was rarely around. He would come into the office for an hour or so after the trucks had gone out in the morning just to check on things and then spend the day out of the office, golfing or riding his Harley or assessing damage that we had done on our moves.

And he was growing a bit weary of doing damage assessments. With winter approaching and Fast Company booking fewer and fewer moves with each passing week, many of the guys started to get lackadaisical and careless. They started grinding out hours (going slow or performing superfluous tasks on the job so that they could extend their time on the clock and make up for the hours they weren't otherwise going to be getting) and apparently taking less care in carrying pieces out the door. Chris had had enough.

So, he scheduled a meeting with us on a Tuesday in mid-November. "Be here at eight o'clock on the dot." We were there, and let me tell you, he let loose. He was livid beyond livid. At first I thought he just needed a hug, but it was more serious than that. That man had a lot of built up anger, and he used that meeting to let it all out. Occupational therapy. And we were all there (on time, front and center) so that we could be present for his tantrum. At one point, I thought I was back in my basketball-playing days at Merrimack College and it was halftime and Coach was giving us his thoughts on how we were playing. There were papers flying, fist pumps, foot stomps, and cursing. Lots and lots of cursing. At times, I couldn't even comprehend what Chris was saying: his sentences were a mere run-on assembly of different tenses of the "F-word," his assurance that we understood how angry he really was. And it was working. He sure got my attention, anyway.

Chris didn't single anyone out, though. He didn't need to. We all knew who was responsible for Chris's displeasure. Grundy had run the roof of the truck into a low lying tree branch ($2,700), Elseto had been scratching the hell out of hardwood floors (almost $4,000), and Michie's crew was averaging about three damaged pieces per week. (Elseto was the only one who was fired after the meeting, but Grundy later came to terms with the fact that the moving business wasn't for him.) But, rather than embarrass anybody in particular, Chris addressed us as a whole. After all, he felt we all needed to shape up or ship out. "You don't like the way we run things around here? You don't like the people you work with? You aren't happy with your paycheck or the fact that you don't have a laundry list of benefits? Fine! Get the hell outta here! I'll run one truck if I have to!"

Chris was passionate about one thing: getting paid. Which was respectable. So what if he made our salaries several times over despite never having to lift a single piece of furniture? He had earned it! With a college education and smart decision-making, he had earned the position that he had attained in life. Good for him. But at the same time, it seemed like he had little or no compassion for what we were going through.

"Shit, that mother ain't never lifted a piece of furniture in his life," one of the guys told me later. "He don't know what it's like for us out there."

And he was right. It wasn't easy for us out there. Moving was hard work, stressful as hell. Carry the buffet out to the truck and come back in for the two-piece China hutch. And then come back for the dining room table and chairs. And then, and then, and then—it seemed endless at times. Ninety-five percent of our moves were local, so it wasn't like we were taking these moves cross-country where we could work hard for four hours and then drive for three days. We worked hard for four hours, drove fifteen minutes, and then worked hard for another three.

If nothing else, Chris's outrage made us tighten up a little bit, but at the same time, it wasn't like Michie's crew was messing up on purpose, and Grundy certainly hadn't meant to damage the roof of the truck. "Hey, look. A tree branch. Think I can knock it down?" It wasn't like that at all. Mistakes were happening—probably more than normal—and Chris simply meant for us to start focusing a little more.

But few cared about what Chris had to say. While we new guys, who were hearing his quarterly speech for the first time, were totally captivated by his words, the guys that had been at Fast Company for any extended period of time could be seen giggling in the corner or staring into space. They'd heard Chris's rant a half-dozen times, and they knew enough by then that things would change for a while and then go back to the way they were. New rule changes ("Be at work by eight o'clock or else!") might last a week, but then guys would resort back to strolling into the shop at 8:30, and no disciplinary action would be taken. Be at work by 8:00 or else what, Chris?

Why, though? Why no respect? Because things weren't like they used to be, like they were when Slugger (Chris's dad) ran the shop.

"It was so different back then, man, when Slugger was here," Victor, a six-year Fast Company employee, told me. "We were a family."

Life with Slugger was more tolerable. He made the guys *want* to get up in the morning and go to work. There is stress in every profession, but in moving, as you can imagine, the stress is multiplied. Every day, we would roll out of bed thinking, "Man, another day of wrapping and lifting and climbing. Damn." That's what we did, six days a week, and it wasn't fun. Some of us did what we could to make it fun, but at the same time, there was nothing easy about what we were doing. Slugger's Fast Company, the Fast Company of yesterday, eased that stress. Chris's Fast Company, today's Fast Company, only added to it.

"Slugger was there for 'his boys,'" Victor told me. "If we came back to the shop having been stiffed on the tip, he would slip us twenty or thirty bucks under the table. We were shooting hoops and putting steaks on the grill in the afternoon."

But when Slugger died of cancer in 2005 and Chris took over, animosity sprung up around the office. Fast Company's reputation suffered, which meant fewer moves, which meant even more animosity at the office. It wasn't just Chris's fault, though. He was trying. A little. On slow days, he might have Pam let movers work around the office or send an extra guy out on a two-man move (at the company's expense) just so they could get hours. He would also organize company outings to local hockey games and restaurants and bowling alleys to try to strengthen the chemistry among us, but it just wasn't the same. He wasn't doing enough at the office. He wasn't there.

"But it's even more than that," another guy offered. "With Slugger, if a customer accused us of damaging something and we said we ain't do it, by God, we ain't do it! He would back us one hundred percent to the point that he would start threatening the customer. 'Dammit! My boys ain't do that! I'll see your ass in court.' It ain't like that with Chris. He just cares about making that paper."

Don't get me wrong, though. I'm not saying we needed more money or we were itching for a health care plan (although both of those would have been fantastic). In fact, not many people that I met during my tenure at Fast Company complained about what they were getting paid. They were just mad at the lack of hands-on leadership. They didn't feel like they belonged to anything. They felt abused. They were robots, sent out to make money for the big boss man, go home, and return and repeat the next day. It was a vicious, destructive cycle, and it hurt the overall morale.

In later conversations, I discovered that even Pam, Chris's mom, felt wholeheartedly that Chris wasn't around enough to run a successful business. "Eight-to-ten," she told me. "He needs to be here in the morning to see the boys off, and then he can go do estimates or damage assessments or play golf or whatever." The proof could be found by comparing the Fast Company in Charleston with the one in Myrtle Beach, which was owned by Chris's brother, Greg. Greg wasn't paying his employees near what Chris was paying us. But, Greg was there, having man-to-man contact with his workers. He would take them out to lunch or hang out with them outside of work. He knew the right buttons to push to keep his employees pumped up, motivated to want to work hard. The morale was at a whole different level than ours.

On the other hand, I can tell you the exact moment when I knew that I had become an official member of the Fast Company crew, the moment that I came to have a sense of affinity.

The pecking order around the shop was separated by one's reputation as a mover. If you were a good mover, then you were a good guy. If you were a bad mover, then you still might have been a good guy, but you were sentenced to the bottom of the hierarchy where you were showered with idle small talk or ignored altogether. (Bad movers, by the way, were either rare at Fast Company or they were assigned to moves where they had to work with each other. The scheduling system was such that the worst movers were weeded out via their own discovery that they simply didn't belong at Fast Company.) For several months, that was me, ignored, but I had stuck with it, thus earning a bit of respect. And one day, I came into the shop, and everybody had a good laugh at my expense.

The topic of conversation surrounded my work attire. Guys at the shelter had already given me plenty of flak about my man-purse, the only tote bag available at the time at the Goodwill, and now it was Fast Company's turn to get on my clothes. From the waist up, I looked normal, donning the standard work shirt that everyone was required to wear on the job. But then there were my shorts, which had, well, earned their name. I had bought about five pairs from the Goodwill to wear on the job, and I got what I paid for: not a single pair of them extended below mid-thigh. And there we were, in the shop, and anybody and everybody was taking shots at me and my sense of style.

"Shep, Daisy Duke called. She wants her shorts back."

Laughter.

"Shep, shouldn't you be wearing something on top of your boxers?"

Laughter.

"Dog, you know what we used to call those in prison? 'Catch me-bang me shorts.'"

Roaring laughter. (Thereafter, my shorts became known as the "catch me's," as in, "Hey, Shep, lookin' good in those catch me's, Buddy.")

They said I looked like the UPS man. Even Amy and Wendy and Pam were having a good time.

So, of course, the UPS guy made an early morning delivery to the office the following week, and of course that man's shorts extended down below his knees. Straight gangster. It was great. It was as if it was meant to happen, as if the chain of events of me being made fun of and his subsequent delivery with his long shorts were supposed to happen. Everybody loved picking on me for my shorts, and I joined right in. I was in. Just as I had climbed the ranks at the shelter (albeit much quicker), that was the week that I discovered that I had become "somebody" at Fast Company. From that point on, I was one of the guys, privileged to join even the most intimate conversations. I never went shopping for new threads, though, partly because they had become my trademark, but mostly since they were so comfortable. I was so agile in those things. I could bend and stretch and move every which way possible. (Although, in January, I did split a pair of shorts—right down the back and right in front of the customer— when I was setting down a TV.)

But just as I came to be accepted by some people, I was having a difficult time dealing with others. Namely, Mike.

Mike was a legend in his own right. Years before, before Curtis had been named Truck Manager, the two of them had worked on the same crew together. They had Mount Pleasant on lockdown—Rivertowne, Snee Farm, Belle Hall, and Dunes West. Every day was a request move for the two of them in the most premiere neighborhoods. Word had gotten around town that those were the two that you wanted to move you. They *were* Fast Company. Their third man was irrelevant. The two of them were the best.

But just as Fast Company's reputation began to founder with Slugger's death, so, too, did the "Mike and Curtis Duo." With a weak back, Curtis was promoted to the office to aid in trying to resurrect what had once been Charleston's number-one local moving company, while Mike jumped from crew to crew, growing more and more bitter every day.

And he was using me as a means to discharge that bitterness— every day on nearly every piece that we would carry together. "Shit man, don't carry it like that! What the hell are you doing? You just aren't cut out for moving." I tried to let his outbursts slide, but then the customers started to feel uncomfortable about the way he was acting, so I had to step in. I approached him on the side, and told him that he would have to shape up a bit. He couldn't keep treating me like that. Fine, I was a terrible mover. "You and Derrick are the best, Mike. Everybody knows that. I want you to teach me your ways, but you can't treat me with such condescension, especially in front of the customers. It's bad for business."

He agreed, but things didn't change, and Derrick told me to make a decision.

"You gotta choose, bro," he told me. "I'm cool with you both, but I can't work with the two of y'all together no more. It's him or me."

In perhaps the easiest decision I'd ever made in my life, I went directly to Pam and told her that I didn't want Mike on my crew anymore. "I know I'm still a nobody in the grand scheme of things here, Pam, but at the same time, I just can't keep working with him. For two months I've been putting up with it, only because I was happy to have Derrick on my crew, but I just can't deal with it anymore."

It turned out that I wasn't the only one. As a matter of fact, I had lasted longer than most of the other people Mike had worked with. He had burned bridges with most of the drivers at Fast Company, which was a shame, since he was such a great mover.

On the outside looking in, what I had done could have been considered a shallow, egocentric move. After all, learning to work with different people was a part of life, right? Screw Derrick and his "him or me" proposition.

But it's not like that in the moving business. Moving is not an equal opportunity occupation. That's how people were getting hurt, sent home with scarred shins, broken fingers, and strained backs. And hernias. Shortly after the new year, Chad, who was super strong and fully capable of carrying whatever was put in front of him, got twisted up on an armoire and tore a hole in his abdominal wall ("The worst pain I ever felt in my life," he said) simply because he wasn't on the same page with the guy that was on the other end. He was out of work for a month (and a month shorter than the doctor had prescribed). Two guys clashing in the moving business was a recipe for disaster, and Derrick's proposition finally gave me the opportunity to get somebody else.

But we didn't get anybody else in particular. We would have a different guy ride with us every day. Didn't matter who.

"You wanna work? Cool. C'mon."

"Uh, they haven't hired me yet."

"Eh, whatever. Let's ride."

A couple of times we even picked up a friend of Derrick's on the way to the customer's house, and once in a while we would do three-man moves by ourselves. It was crazy. One day, I was dropping pieces and falling off the truck ramp and scraping walls, and the next day I was a legit mover, carrying heavy pieces, clearing rooms by myself, and scraping walls. Customers that were looking at us at the start of the day like, "Um, where are the real movers? Y'know, the big guys?" would have ear-to-ear smiles on their faces at the end of the day when we would beat their estimated time by two or three hours. Derrick and I were even getting requested every couple of weeks.

The best part about it, though, wasn't getting rid of Mike. I would have dealt with him forever, as long as Derrick was out there with us. The best part was the fact that Derrick, rather than taking the easy road and jumping ship, wanted to stay with me. And that was awesome. Some crews had been together for years and some crews would only last two or three months before they dissolved. And it was looking like Derrick and I were going to last.

After Thanksgiving, my predetermined two-month window to live at Mickey's place downtown was nearing its end. I could have stayed there forever if I wanted to (I know Mickey loved getting $100 a week for his otherwise vacant attic), but that's not what I wanted. I wanted something more permanent, with a bed and my own kitchen and a living room. Maybe even a community pool and a tennis court and a nice view of the Cooper River. Finding a roommate was going to be the easy part, though. I did a little research at the website Roommates. com and found a horde of people in the Charleston area looking for people to live with.

But just as I had compiled a hefty list of prospective roommates, Derrick told me all about Bubble Gum, and my roommate search came to an end.

THIRTEEN

WINTER WITH BUBBLE GUM

〜✦〜

After Thanksgiving, my project continued on its evolutionary path, but it also began to shift to more of a cultural one. Especially after I met my new roommate.

He got the nickname "Bubble Gum" when he was a kid. One of his cousins told him that his puffy cheeks made him look like his mouth was stuffed with bubble gum, and the name stuck. But now people only called him that when they were mad at him, like a mom using her son's entire name for emphasis. Everybody called him BG.

He was Derrick's cousin, and he had arrived unexpectedly at Derrick's front doorstep in mid-October from their native Kingstree, about an hour from Charleston. Kingstree is a rural, backwoods town with its own flavor and atmosphere where one can always find excitement at places like Mirage—soul food restaurant by day, dance club by night. But just as Kingstree's social scene is hot, the center of all of the surrounding country towns, the economy is cold, not offering much in the way of jobs or opportunity. Everybody has his or her own business and everybody's business is in the red. BG had grown tired of working as a cook at his aunt's restaurant, and he was looking for a change of scenery, the type of change that Derrick had experienced when he came to Charleston three years prior.

Just like Derrick, BG had an average physical appearance. He wasn't tall or muscle-bound or extremely athletic. He did have a perpetual look of contemplation on his face, though, like he was always looking for something intelligent to say. Sometimes he even mumbled to himself, regardless of who was around. Often, very often in fact, I would wonder what was going through his head during idle moments in conversation.

BG was on the hunt for a roommate. He didn't care who, and neither did Derrick. Derrick just wanted him out. He had given BG until December to get on his feet and find another place to live, so that his two-year-old daughter could have her room back.

Enter me.

From the moment that I met BG two days after Thanksgiving, we had a love-hate relationship—from which most of the love would be expended in the first couple of days. We were so much alike—stubborn and contentious—so we were at odds from the beginning. But even though we didn't exactly hit it off, being roommates was such a convenient opportunity for each of us. He needed a roommate, I needed a roommate, and the duplex next door to Derrick needed occupants.

We went down to the realtor's office to check on the availability, and the agent seemed stunned by our inquiry.

"Wait, you mean four oh nine *B* Pine Hollow, like over in *Cedar Manor*?" she asked.

"Yep, that's the one."

"Are you sure?"

"Yeah, why?"

"Oh, wow. Have you been inside yet?"

You know it's bad when even the realtor is skeptical about one of her own properties. Boy was I having bad luck with living quarters.

The shelter and even Mickey's attic were necessary, but I had dealt with those conditions with the optimistic notion that I could find something halfway decent by December. But it wasn't looking good.

Four oh nine B Pine Hollow was a step down, once again, from where I had been living. It had been on the market for four months since the previous tenants—a family of grizzly bears, I believe—had moved out. There were roaches and piles of trash everywhere. The linoleum in the kitchen was ripped and the stove was rusted. There were holes and stains on the carpet throughout, and the walls were in dire need of a paint job. It looked like Mama Bear had let Baby Bear loose in the house with a jug of cherry Kool-Aid and a box of crayons. It was horrendous. I couldn't imagine that anybody would seriously consider renting that place.

They were desperate to rent the property, which was great, because we were desperate to find one. It gave everybody a little breathing room. We told the realtor that if she went easy on the credit check and supplied us with paint, we would have that place looking habitable again. It was a deal fit for everybody, although I spent most of the negotiation process hoping and praying that BG had a tangible plan for how we were going to actually implement the masterminded makeover that we were so gallantly proposing to the realtor.

After reaching an agreement, but before we could move in, there was a lot of work to be done on our duplex. The only problem, though, was that BG was handy—super handy, like the fellas that have their own TV shows on Sunday mornings—and I wasn't. It wasn't a *huge* problem, except that BG wouldn't let me forget how handy he was and how handy I wasn't.

"Dog, I gotta ask you. What the hell are you doing?"

I was patching the drywall.

"Oh, Jesus. Shep, please, I'm beggin' you. Grab a paint brush and go over there in the corner. I got everything else." He waved his hand around the whole apartment, signaling that he was going to take care of everything except that one corner to which I had been assigned.

I think he wished I had given him $100 and just left him to perform all of the renovations himself. I didn't have a clue what I was doing patching the drywall, but I wasn't good at painting either. Since the realtor hadn't provided us with carpet protector, I would spend ten minutes painting and then a half hour scrubbing white paint off the carpet. I hated it. As imperative as it was, I hated *all* of the work we were putting into that hideous place, but I really hated painting. BG knew what he was doing, though, and I didn't, so I had to comply.

Derrick came over to deliver cookies from his wife and to pick up my slack, which helped to expedite the process. After one weekend of non-stop work, we had that place gleaming. It was great. Our own place. Even the things we couldn't fix, like holes in the carpet, we strategically planned to cover with furniture. We had it all mapped out.

My bedroom (the master) was in the back of the duplex, and I paid proportionately more for it. Our rent was $600, so I told BG that I would pay $325 and he could pay $275, and he agreed enthusiastically. I could have gotten off with a much better deal than that, but it was fair for everybody. I wanted the bigger room and he was saving for a car, so it would give him a chance to put a few extra dollars in the bank.

Moving in was an unexciting affair, though. We hardly had anything. He had a bed, and I had a bed that I had scored from a move, but other than that, we just put our clothes in the closet, and dreamed up the interior plan for our new place.

"We'll put a sofa here and a sofa there and a TV there," he told me.

"Yeah, yeah. And we can put a china cabinet here, maybe a bookshelf or something on that wall."

"Or no, wait. China cabinet there and a wine rack over there."

We weren't being sarcastic. We were serious, and our plan was certainly plausible. BG was going to start working at Fast Company, too, so we would both have access to furniture. Before, Derrick and I had been turning down the used TVs and furniture that were being offered to us almost daily by our customers, or we had been taking them to the pawnshop ("If it ain't broke, sell it to somebody."). Now that we had a place to put things, BG and I could start accepting the pieces for our own. Beautiful pieces. If you're ever trying to furnish a house or apartment, go work as a mover. Derrick's place and his sister's place around the corner were both filled with hand-me-downs from customers, so BG and I knew that it wouldn't be long before our place would be filled as well. And we were right. Within a month, 409B Pine Hollow was fully furnished with a beautiful cream-colored sectional sofa, a maroon sleeper sofa, a fifty-five-inch projection TV (which cost $300), a bookshelf, a dining room table (although we never got chairs), and a china hutch. In my bedroom, I had two nightstands, a dresser, a TV, a bookshelf, and a huge desk—all free and all in December. None of it matched, so our house looked thrown together, but individually each piece was beautiful.

Even my bedroom came together nicely. I had picked up a wide variety of interior decorating tips from the customers we had moved, so I was pretty much a pro. I hung pictures and candles and a clock over my desk. I splurged for a $65 burgundy and white bedspread set, which was complemented by the matching burgundy lampshades and white candles that I put on top of my nightstands and a burgundy and white rug that I bought from Target. My bathroom—from the towels to the shower curtain to the candles—was a sea of Carolina blue and white. It was immaculate, pristine. The whole place. We should have called HGTV to come film the entire process of restoration. With BG's expertise and my moral support, we were cruising. After the New Year, we would acquire rugs and side tables to finish off the living room. Later, even after our place was completely outfitted, BG continued accepting pieces, so our kitchen and back porch filled up with sofas and cabinets that we never used but he didn't feel right letting go to waste.

BG's street smarts—particularly in his own mind—far outweighed his lacking academic expertise. He hadn't finished high school, but that didn't matter much to him. He was still right. About everything. All the time. Even when somebody would say he was wrong, he knew he was wrong, and there was clear, concrete evidence that he was wrong, he still fought for his point. "I'm tellin' you, man, I been around more than you. I seen more than you. I know what I'm talkin' about." Even on those rare occasions that he was downright 100 percent wrong, he would discount the argument altogether. "Dog, why you even worried about it? It ain't that serious."

In an effort to prove his point, he loved incorporating clichés into his argument. Unfortunately for him, though, he would frequently misuse them or create his own philosophical rendition, thus leaving his audience even more confused. When he would talk about not counting something valuable before you have it, he would say, "Ha! See. That's what you get when your chickens done hatched, but you ain't count 'em yet." Or one time, we were talking about turning a minor issue into a major one, and he said, "Shit. You already got plenty of molehills. You might as well build your own mountain. You know what I'm sayin'?" Hmmmm. Derrick and I would ask him if he really meant "make a mountain out of a molehill," but he would just shrug it off. "Y'all don't get it. Never mind."

Apparently, he had plenty of people that did get it, though. BG had a thousand friends, and most of them lived in our neighborhood. I know, because there was always somebody knocking on our door, at all times of the day. "Is BG here? No? Mind if I come in and chill until he gets back?" Everybody loved BG, seeing him as someone who wasn't intimidating to be around. In social settings, he was fun and easy-going and always good for a laugh. BG and I could sit around and have the most ridiculous discussions, and in the end, he would have me lying on the couch curled up in laughter.

With that said, however, the first month with BG was tough. We weren't on the same page as far as getting the place squared away. I had a few extra dollars that I wanted to put toward communal items like dishes, pots and pans, cleaning supplies, and decorative items for the living room, but he didn't want to splurge. He was a cheapskate, he knew it, and he didn't care. So, I had to buy everything, which wasn't a huge deal beyond the principle that I had wanted to establish in getting us in the habit of pulling our own weight. I should have fought harder in the beginning, because for the duration of our time as roommates, I was always the one buying paper towels or dish liquid and he was always the one "borrowing" toilet paper or a glass of milk. He would spend $15 a day or more on cigarettes and beer and lottery tickets, but he never had a bar of soap.

BG was having a tough time working his way in with the management at Fast Company. His attitude was varied. One week he was on fire, going in to the shop ready to work, but then the next week he was a completely different person.

And that's how it was with so many of the guys at work. Rarely did a day go by without some sort of drama in the shop in the morning.

Some of the guys had a good attitude, while others fueled the two-way turmoil between the management and the employees.

Some guys got in to the shop early, got their work orders, and hit the road. Others arrived at the shop close to 9:00 AM—the time when we were supposed to arrive at the customer's house. Others, still, would be on the schedule and wouldn't show up. No call, no message; just wouldn't feel like working that day.

Some came in uniform, ready to work, while others constantly tested the system.

What was Chris, the owner, going to do? Fire them? Not a chance. It would cost him more money to fire a mover, hire a new one, and then train him than it would to just accept the lack of respect that he was getting from certain employees.

Derrick was always looking out for BG, so, after a while, in mid-December, he invited BG to join our crew at Fast Company. BG wasn't getting the hours he wanted by floating around from crew to crew, and since he knew that he would get sent out pretty much every day with us, he jumped at the opportunity when Derrick offered it to him.

And it was awful from the start. It's tough to work and live together, spending nearly all of your waking moments with somebody. It was good that Derrick was there to keep us separated, but the moving experience, in general, wasn't the same as before. Derrick and I had been on a roll, and when BG came in, he started to get in the way. Talent-wise, he was a good mover, but his work ethic was poor. Terrible. There Derrick and I were, running around loading pieces on the truck, and there was BG, loafing from the truck to the house. He didn't care. Hell, the slower he went, the more hours he got, and he knew that his own cousin wasn't going to get rid of him, no matter how unhurried he was.

So, for the next two months, it was Adam and the Kingstree boys—one day at a time. Things weren't the same and Derrick knew it. He swore every day that he was either going to kick BG into high gear or kick him off the crew, but in reality he was helping BG get as many hours as possible. I never hid my discontent, but at the same time, I couldn't be mad at the hours we were getting, even in the slow season. Derrick knew he was doing me wrong, and he went to Pam to tell her to give me a raise, so by the middle of December, I was making $10 an hour and gliding through the winter on cruise control just like everybody else.

Our place was vacant for the twenty-fourth through the twenty-sixth of December. BG went to be with his brothers and his mom in Kingstree for Christmas, while I headed up Interstate 95 to Raleigh where I was greeted with stark revelation.

First, my friends and family, who I had not seen in five months, discovered—and made their feelings known to me—that not all movers are husky. I tried to tell them that muscle-bound movers are that way because they lifted weights or because they had recently completed a three-year stint upstate where they had been doing hundreds of push-ups and pull-ups and sit-ups in their prison cell every day. But they didn't want to hear it. They figured I was going to come home having gone through a Hulk-like transformation, but that just wasn't the case. As a matter of fact, with my rigorous lifestyle and poor diet, I had actually lost weight, so I was even scrawnier than I had been before I departed for Charleston. Nobody was impressed.

Secondly, my pops was grossly disappointed in my attempt at growing a goatee, something I had been working on since I had entered the shelter in July in an effort to try to fit in. Whereas the beards donning the faces of the some of the other guys with whom I had been associated could have made very generous donations to Locks of Love, my facial hair was scraggly and sparse. I was a victim of genetics, and my pops told me that my face just looked dirty.

Finally, I realized how serious my current project really was, how immersed I had become. Bound for Raleigh late in the evening of December 23, I had left my furnished duplex in Charleston wearing my new clothes, driving my new truck home for the two days that Fast Company had given me off. I paid for gas and food with money, new money that had come from my new life, all having sprouted from my $25 seed money. Months prior in July, I had given all of my personal belongings—clothes, furniture, books, everything—to my brother, and after my year was complete, I would go on with my life with the money and goods that I had acquired in Charleston. It was an eye-opener. It's so satisfying to look back after one, two, ten, or forty years at what you've accomplished. "Man, those were the good ol' days." *These!* Right now! *These* are the good ol' days. I was savoring every moment, the roots of my future. Who knows if I would succeed in achieving my predetermined goals or not, but that didn't matter so much to me. Thinking back to my first night in July when I stepped off the train in North Charleston, I realize how naïve I was, how I didn't know how to get there, necessarily, but I knew where I was going. Just me and a dream. In the end, though, isn't it really more about the journey, the process; about setting goals, finding something you're passionate about, and giving it all you've got? Isn't it, as BG would say, about "shooting for the stars; even if you miss, you'll land among the moon?"

After the New Year, my life really started to take shape. With a truck, a furnished apartment, and forty-hour workweeks, I was well ahead of where I thought I was going to be after just five or six months.

We all have our vices, though. For some, it's alcohol or drugs. Maybe gambling or adultery for others. Fortunately, I was able to keep mine—the greasy buffet at Mama D's Dirty South Barbecue on Dorchester Road—under control by eating there just once a week on Sundays. For the most part, in fact, my new eating habits were a huge change for the better. I was preparing my own breakfast and packing sandwiches and trail mix for lunch. I was really starting to save money, and I was eating right at the same time. BG would inquire about the dinner recipe for the evening, and then he would shake his head and take off for Burger King or Arby's, so the kitchen was mine to concoct whatever kind of creations I could come up with. If there was one distinct advantage I had in completing this project, it was that I could eat chicken and Rice-A-Roni for every meal, every day. I love it and there's not much I can do about it. I mean, what's not to like? Chicken is chicken and can be cooked ten thousand different ways, and Rice-A-Roni is just absolutely delicious. For about a dollar, I could whip up two generous portions of "The San Francisco Treat," one for now, one for later. Sure, I could have saved a few bucks if I would have purchased a fifty-pound bag of white rice with my new Sam's Club membership, but there is simply no way to substitute for those flavor packets inside the box. They're unequaled. Spanish Rice, Parmesan and Romano Cheese, Beef, Whole Grain Roasted Garlic Italiano, Chicken and Herb, Fried Rice—there are like a hundred different flavors. Joined with a new chicken recipe and a can of corn or green beans, every night was a feast. And that wasn't even the best part. In just one box of Broccoli Au Gratin Rice-A-Roni (unquestionably the best flavor) I was getting a healthy serving of carbohydrates, thiamine, and folic acid. All that *and* nearly 100 percent of my daily value of sodium! You can't beat that.

I was quickly learning the value of a dollar, too. Early on living at 409B Pine Hollow, I realized why my youth had been filled with scoldings from my mom to "Close the door or I'm gonna forward you the electric bill! What are you tryin' to do, air condition the great outdoors?" On January 9, the electric bill came, and it was crazy. Crazy to the tune of $209 for our two-bedroom duplex, just for the month of December. BG was already sensitive to spending a dollar on anything he didn't deem absolutely necessary, so he was particularly annoyed when we got the electric bill. He spent the entire month of January making sure all of the doors and windows were shut tight and lights were off in the house. I liked where his head was at, but at times, it was getting to be a little too much.

"Dog, what did I tell you about keepin' the lights on?" he asked me one night.

"Dude, I'm cookin' dinner in here."

"I don't give a shit. Them lights cost. Cook during the day. I tell you what, we're just gonna each start paying for every time we have a light on. I'm gonna keep track."

So, he walked around with a notepad for the next two days before he realized that his math skills weren't up to par. But we understood what we had to do. We started smartening up about our energy usage and by the end of January, our bill was back down around $125 where it was supposed to be. As a matter of fact, we were conserving across the board—water, laundry detergent, dish liquid, toiletries. Everything costs, and we did everything we could to keep our costs down.

My only big splurge was a gym membership at East Shore Athletic Club, which, at less than $43 per month, was well worth it. I had access to nautilus and cardio equipment, free weights, racquetball, pool, sauna, whirlpool … everything. Aside from lifting furniture, which was made so much easier by Fast Company's method of wheeling pieces out the door, I hadn't done any kind of physical activity with my upper body in six months, and it was starting to show. My arms were thinning out and my belly was getting pudgy, and, more importantly, I didn't feel good. (Interestingly, though, my legs and back were as powerful as they had ever been in my life.) The gym offered me an outlet, away from the stress of the real world, if only for forty-five minutes or an hour and, also, an opportunity to start to buff up for the summer.

Which was important, because after the New Year, my social life started to catch fire. Well, kind of. I gave LD's—the dance club where BG was a member—a try, but I was all but banished (mostly laughed at) after just one trip at the hands of my sub-par dancing abilities. It turns out that somewhere along the way, somebody decided that dancing ("grinding," the kids call it these days) should be confined to one's movement of just his or her hips with limited movement of the rest of his or her body. Screw that. If I'm going to bring it, I'm coming with everything. Head to toe. So, I was banished to the downtown area—not by any means a boring place to hang out—where my dancing skills would be more widely accepted. That is, I could blend in with much bigger crowds that wouldn't much notice my arms flailing about or my robot-like movements to and fro (although some of my moves were still weeded out over the weeks at the hands of their own unpopularity. My favorite series was virtually eliminated on the spot when a very attractive girl told me—half-joking—that it looked like I was doing aerobics). I was never a heavy drinker, which would have only improved my deficient dancing skills, I'm sure, so my weekend excursions were never expensive, but, at the same time, a very necessary escape from the tension of my daily life.

BG could fix anything, which turned out to be our bonding point, the time we really got along. It was his time to show off. If anything needed repair, he was right there, on the job, ready to fix it. His abilities were useful around the house when the dishwasher was broken or the toilets were backed up beyond the help of a plunger or we had to install the washer and dryer set that Derrick had rented to us for a year.

Even better, his handyman skills particularly applied to automobiles, which turned out to work very well for both of us. He was short on cash all the time and my truck was making a different noise all the time. There was a noise for speeds under thirty miles per hour, a noise for speeds over sixty miles per hour, and a noise for the speeds in between. Squeaks, rattles, thumps. Here a noise, there a noise, always a noise. More than once, the lady at the drive-through at Taco Bell made me turn off my truck so she could hear me place my order.

But BG could always diagnose the problem, usually just by the sound.

"Ah, shit, man. That's your motor support. I can fix that. No problem."

"Cool."

"For fifty dollars."

And he would fix it. No problem. I mean, I could have been forking over much more than $50 at a time to make each repair, but I didn't need to. It was money well-earned on his part and money well-spent on mine.

On the flip side, he rarely cleaned the house, though. The only time he would clean was every other weekend when he had a girl coming over to hang out. She didn't know it, but she was getting the royal treatment. Our place would be disgusting before her arrival, after I had pretty much given up being the only one vacuuming and mopping and washing dishes and taking out the trash. But then one day, I would come back from the store and all of a sudden there was BG in the kitchen, sweating, working harder than he ever did at Fast Company.

"Adam, can you give me a hand, man. Quick. Sheena's coming over in like a half hour."

Our place would be spotless for the next week or so until I grew tired, once again, of keeping the place maintained, but then BG would make plans with another chick, and he would get back to washing and mopping. I even thought about paying a girl every now and then to come hang out with BG, just to keep the place clean—kind of like a maid service—but I didn't need to. BG was doing quite well for himself moving furniture by day, skirt-chasing by night.

It was good that he had an entourage of women in his life, because he was somehow always getting himself into a pickle with at least one of them. My all-time favorite BG experience happened in early February. He was talking on the phone with Marisol, one of his girls from Kingstree, and he was "spittin' crazy game."

"So, wassup, girl, all fine and shit. You gonna come over or what?"

It didn't appear that she was in the mood for an eleven o'clock booty call, but BG was fighting hard nonetheless. He was putting in a lot of work when a beep came in on the phone.

"Hey, girl. Hold on one second. I got another call comin' in. I'll be right back ... Hello?"

It was Sheniya, his main girl.

"Oh, wassup, girl. All fine and shit. You gonna come through tonight or what?"

He spent thirty seconds or so feeding the same lines to Sheniya that he had just been feeding to Marisol. This was classic already, but his woes were just getting started. When he clicked back over, Marisol asked him who was on the other line.

"Oh, that was just my bro, checkin' in. Y'know. Family business."

"Really?" she said. "Interesting. So that wasn't Sheniya, and you didn't just tell her ..."

Marisol recited the exact conversation that BG had just had with Sheniya. BG glanced, confused, at his phone and then he glanced at me with the same look.

"What?" I asked.

"Ah, damn," he said.

Instead of hitting the "switch" button on the phone to click over, BG had hit the "link" button, thus turning the call into a three-way conversation. Marisol had heard everything, and there wasn't much he could do from that point. For the first time in his womanizing career, BG was stuck. He spent the rest of the night trying to talk his way out, including putting me on the phone to vouch for his character, but Marisol didn't want to hear it. She didn't ever want to talk to him again.

Until a day later, when BG cooked her dinner. Then everything was good. And the house was clean.

Acts like that kept me constantly amazed at the unpredictability of living with BG, in an environment that I wasn't used to. Each stage in the previous six months had brought on something new and different, something unexpected. Each progression upward had brought on new opportunity, new people, new attitudes, new conflict, and new resolutions. I mean, I never could have guessed when I first agreed to room with BG that there would be a direct correlation between his sociability and the cleanliness of our house. That was startling to me, but at the same time, it was his way of life. We had to compromise on so many levels. Just as he had to get used to me cooking dinner at night with the lights on, I had to get used to him forgetting leftovers in the microwave. We made sacrifices so that we could get along, and for the most part, we did. We had felt out each other's personalities during the month of December and by January, we knew how to handle each other.

FOURTEEN

CULTURE SHOCKED

❧

The greatest part about moving was the end of the day. As is the case in so many professions, it was so gratifying to look over what we had done. Every day, after settling the bill, we would hobble through the house to the truck, exhausted, with a smile on our faces. "We did that."

Even after the moves where we only moved three pieces—especially after the three-piece moves, actually—the gratification would still be there. Three-piece moves were always the most burdensome, particularly since two or three would typically be assigned in one day. Nobody called Fast Company to move a few pieces unless those pieces were massive: ten-foot, two-piece bookshelves, fireproof file cabinets, safes, pianos, and armoires.

One time, Derrick and I got sent out on the "two-hour mini" from hell to move one piece (a bulky 375-pound oak and leather desk) down three flights of stairs and up another three. I was perturbed and confused at the same time. Why oak? Why not pine? Pine is grossly underrated, at least from a mover's point of view. Lightweight, durable, stylish. And leather? I want to meet that man, the man that looked at a cow and thought, "Well, I do need somewhere to put my computer." But, in the end, after you move a desk like that up the stairs, without a scratch on it, it's worth it. You feel superhuman, like one of those Russian behemoths you see on TV competing to be the strongest man in the world. You want to strap an eighteen-wheeler to your back and pull it down the street and then carry one hundred-kilogram anvils up the stairs—in each arm—for absolutely no reason other than to say, "Look at what a beast I am." Egos thrive (or die) in the world of moving. Even with Derrick carrying his end of that desk up the stairs with ease and me wobbling around like a newborn colt testing my land legs, it was still quite fulfilling.

And so were the longer moves. Generally, our moves would average around eight hours, but every now and then, one would go eleven or twelve if we were sent out to Kiawah or Seabrook Island where we would move one mansion around the corner to another, newly constructed mansion. Those moves usually required two or three trips, even with the way Derrick strategically packed the truck tight and to the ceiling.

But then came the eighteen-and-a-half-hour move, the move that marked my rite of passage as a mover.

We were on Daniel Island, which is truly a world all its own. Live there, stay there. Jan Sully, or "Mizz Sully," had what we call in the moving biz "an assload of stuff." When we did the walk-through, we couldn't believe it. You could tell from the looks on our faces that we didn't know how we were ever going to be able to complete that move. Her house had room after room after room. Her kitchen was larger than our apartment, and the master bedroom had a living room. And each room was loaded with boxes and furniture and mattresses. Then, when we went outside by the pool, we were greeted by enough lawn furniture to host a party of fifty of her friends' closest friends. It was incredible.

"Well, ma'am, this is a monster move," I told her. "It's going to take a good bit of time."

She laughed at me. One, single, hardcore, sarcastic laugh. And then she led us to the garage.

I wasn't upset at the fact that her two-car garage was filled to the ceiling. I wasn't upset that she could have furnished a nine thousand square foot house (which she had done, in fact, when she lived in New Jersey, "just two houses down from Terrell Owens," the football star) with everything she had crammed into her current four thousand square foot dwelling. I wasn't even upset that she had gotten her full money's worth on the tall wardrobe boxes by stuffing the bottoms with shoes and linens. I was just upset that she was so much like my own mom, unable to throw anything away, ever. "Oh, dear, can't throw that away," Mizz Sully would say. "That was the first (*enter item of your choice*) that Gerald and I ever bought. Sentimental value, you know." I could understand photo albums and pictures that her daughter had drawn when she was four years old. Her son's first baseball mitt or a pair of his baby shoes? Fino. But this lady had taken it to another level. She had saved every shirt, blanket, dish, and book that she had ever come across. She had *six* garden hoses. I couldn't believe all the stuff she had.

And most of it was in mint condition, untarnished. She had $13 less than God, and she wanted to make sure we knew it. "Guys, please, please, please. Be careful with this. It cost twenty four hundred dollars. It can't be replaced." She would have loathed raising me. "See, that's why we don't have nice things," was my mom's tagline. Mizz Sully's lawn chairs had a higher resale value than my pickup truck, and her indoor furniture was all antique and pretty much in its original condition. I even felt bad washing my hands with the elegantly designed bar of soap in the bathroom.

It didn't help my mental preparation for the day that I was with two guys that I had never worked with. Derrick was house-shopping with his wife, so he had taken the day off, but he had already achieved his rite of passage as a mover. The summer before my arrival, he had completed a twenty-four-hour move—a full day, literally. The lady he moved had started crying, telling him that she absolutely had to be out of the house before the next morning, no other option, so they had worked straight through the night until 8:30 the following day. Now, it was my turn.

The first truckload was a cinch. We took mostly boxes from the garage and the lawn furniture and headed over to Mizz Sully's new place—five minutes away—where most of the boxes went into the garage and the lawn furniture went around back. No stairs on the first trip. The ensuing loads weren't going to be as easy, though. On the way back to load up the second round, we rode in silence. We couldn't believe what we were facing, that we had just only begun. Most of the rest of her stuff was heavy, and we were not excited about it.

But, then something crazy happened. Almost miraculously, we got in "the zone." All three of us, at the same time, five minutes into the second load. It was as if all of our minds telepathically connected and said, "Welp, this crap ain't gonna move itself, fellas. Might as well get going."

We got into a mode where we wouldn't stop, couldn't stop. We were moving independently of our own objective thought. It was as if our bodies were there, moving, but our minds were elsewhere, lost. We knew what we had to do and we did it—subconsciously, for the rest of the day. From noon until 3:30 AM, we moved Mizz Sully's belongings with only one short break for dinner. I was so out of it by 3:30 that I was still ready to go back for more. My body had been shut down for hours, numbed to the effects of heaving furniture, and I knew that I wouldn't feel it until the next day. I knew about "the zone" from playing sports, and Derrick and I had even gotten into "the zone" on moves before but on a much smaller scale. We would be carrying so many pieces at such a fast pace that an hour or two would become a free flow of energy, a free flow of boxes and wood and appliances. But the eighteen-and-a-half-hour move was a different level, the longest job of my moving career. And I was very grateful that I had that experience. Every move I did after that was a picnic, a walk in the park compared to that move. Every time I would be struggling to fight through a move that I just didn't want to be on, I would just think back to Mizz Sully's house. "Could be worse." It was similar to moving when it rained: rainy days sucked, but they made us appreciate the sunny days even more; bad tips made us appreciate the good ones; carrying a piano or a Trinitron TV made everything else appear feather-light. The gratification from completing Mizz Sully's move would last a long time. Derrick had been telling me about his twenty-four-hour move for quite some time—how he had taken only one fifteen-minute break, napping on the bathroom sink, and how he had to call a few of his friends at midnight to replace the other guys on the move—but I didn't really appreciate the full effect of his stories until I had one of my own to tell.

By the time the three of us got back to the shop after 4:00 AM and hobbled home by 4:30, we only got a couple hours of sleep before it was time to go back to do it all over again. At least I didn't have to warm up the truck the next morning.

I got sick in February. Really sick. Looking for a cultural experience without going abroad, I had eaten five ninety-nine-cent tacos from one of the van-restaurants on the side of the road on Rivers Avenue, and the ingredients evidently hadn't met many of the same health regulations that a normal restaurant would have to meet. My whole body hurt for a week straight, but mostly my entrails were turning somersaults. It was the biggest setback of my entire journey, only because it lasted seven days, and I didn't have any way to get treatment. I probably should have been laid up in a hospital, or, at the very least, at home resting, but I couldn't afford to miss work. I didn't have a family physician, obviously, or health insurance, and one trip to a doc-in-a-box cost $95 plus whatever I would have to pay for antibiotics, none of which was a feasible option. (It wasn't until a month later that I learned about the free health clinic.) I loaded up on Maalox and other over-the-counter medicines—necessary expenses that chipped away at my savings account—and I ate everything that the *Doctor's Book of Home Remedies* at Barnes and Noble told me to. By day four, all of my symptoms had pointed directly to having a stomach ulcer—the result of my consumption of some harmful Latin-named bacteria—so at least I knew what I had to treat. Nevertheless, it was a painful experience that had me falling behind on our moves. Way behind. Derrick tolerated it for two days but then had me work with somebody else until I felt better. No sympathy.

BG saw that I was hurting, so he gave me a few days off from our constant bickering. But at the first sign of my feeling better, we picked up right where we had left off.

We always argued. It was like a sport to us, our recreational activity. Literally. That's how we burned calories at night. If we weren't bickering, then something wasn't right, which wasn't necessarily a bad thing since everything was out there, in the open, no holds barred. And 99 percent of the time, our feuds were so trivial, anyway, that we never took each other seriously.

"Man, BG. What is this? I just bought this box of Frosted Flakes yesterday. How's it empty already?"

"Chill, Shep. I was hungry and I couldn't get to the store."

"Right. But the whole box?"

"Dog, why you even worried about it?"

"I'm just sayin', I just hate that you eat all my food, all the time. Sandwiches, chicken, cereal. But, whatever. Just forget about it. You need to save your money anyway, so you can afford to buy wholesale packages of Chap Stick for your big-ass lips."

"My lips, huh? Dog, look at your ears. Dumbo. Yo' goofy ass got the biggest ears I ever seen in my life. Them bitches are like satellite dishes. Shit, go stand by the TV and see if you can fix some of that static."

Such was our conversation, at least once a day. We would then retreat to our neutral corners for a couple of hours until BG needed a favor.

"Hey, man, can I borrow your truck to run up to the gas station right quick?"

"Sure, here's a dollar. Grab me a Mountain Dew."

"Cool."

I wondered which gas station he was going to, though. Maybe the one down in Savannah. He would be gone for at least three hours—usually more like five—and that would tick me off even more, so our dissension would begin anew upon his return. It was a relentless cycle, but somehow it was never very serious. Quick to quarrel, quick to make amends.

In spite of our clashes, BG and I were still becoming friends. His life had been so much more interesting than mine, and I loved hearing about it. Especially his time in jail. His stories frequently started with, "Shoot, this food is a'ight. But it ain't as good as the food up at Effin'ham They food you right up there." Or, "Man, I remember this one time up in Kingstree ..." Unlike a lot of people he knew—like Derrick, who had served twenty-four months—he had never done any hard time in prison. Even BG's brother was serving hard time for an arson conviction. He had gotten into an argument with a lady who had made prejudiced remarks, and he told her he was going to burn down her flower shop. So, he did. But BG knew better than to make stupid decisions like that. His violations were always minor—getting locked up for driving with a suspended license or for beating up his stepfather "in self-defense" when BG heard he was assaulting his mom. Or my favorite, the time he went to Bike Week up in Myrtle Beach, which was jam packed with the biggest and baddest motorcyclists on the East Coast riding the biggest and baddest motorcycles in the world. BG rented a moped, and was "actin' a fool" on the strip. Among thousands of men showing off their hogs, there was BG showing off his moped. "I was lucky the cops got me befo' one of them Billy Badasses did," he told me. BG had a personal relationship with mischief, which had left him with many stories to tell and many more to create.

It seemed like that was the case with everybody in our neighborhood. Everybody was up to something. There was so much culture and flavor in our house just about every night. And you pretty much always knew what everybody was thinking, since few people held anything back.

That's how it was when I met Bonesy, a friend of Derrick and BG's who lived eight houses down from us. He was always showing up at our front stoop asking for a favor. He was a loudmouth with a heavy Brooklyn accent, just as wide as he was short, who had a reputation for speaking his mind. His speech, somehow, was eloquent and scholarly almost, but with a gangster twist. "Dog, I gotta tell ya. I just believe that you didn't think through the ramifications of your actions beforehand. Nah mean?" (To which BG would reply, "B, what'd I tell you about using words like 'ramfications'?")

I'll never forget the first time I met Bonesy. I had a monstrous cold sore on my lip, which everybody else was politely ignoring, but Bonesy wasn't so kind. And once he got going, he didn't stop until *he* was tired of listening to himself talk.

"Dog, what the *fuck* is that on your lip? Son, please, tell me. I gotta know. That shit is real aggressive. You get in a fight? You burn yourself? It looks like it has a mind of its own. I feel like we should distinguish it as a separate body part or at least give it a name. Do you put a leash around it and take it for a walk when you wake up in the morning? I don't know whether to sit down and write an ode to it or grab a fly swatter and try to kill it. It doesn't bite, does it? BG, go get some bug spray. I wanna pop it, but I don't want to catch that shit, too. It's not airborne is it? Dog, if I was your roommate, I'd have you quarantined. I was gonna try to bring some broads over tonight, but you can forget all that. You need to just buy some medicine and go to your room for a few days until that shit disappears. Unbelievable. That thing is real aggressive. And look right there. I think it's having babies. Damn. That sucks. An entire herpes family on your lip. Dog, go to your room ..."

He continued without taking a breath but, lost amid a cloud of laughter, I couldn't absorb the rest of his tirade. By the end, BG had literally fallen over, partly at what Bonesy was saying and partly at the shock on my face from being introduced to him in such a manner. One of the guys that had come over with Bonesy was looking at the ground, merely shaking his head. "Aaaaats Bonesy!" Everybody needs a guy like him in their life, to keep things honest, and I was happy we had him as a part of the crew. He was the guy that would say what everybody else was thinking and, ironically, didn't care what anybody else thought.

The biggest surprise of my time in Charleston was how happy we were. Of course we all had bills and family issues and other stress to deal with, just like everybody else in the world, but we—Derrick, BG, and whoever else was around—always found time for good times. We couldn't afford the luxuries of going out to eat at elegant restaurants during the week or going to theme parks on the weekend, but we found happiness in simple pleasures. I've already mentioned my dancing escapades downtown, which became, at least by the looks I would get, more of a spectacle than anything else. "Who's the tall, lanky kid, and why is he moving around like that?" But there was still plenty of fun to be had on the north end of town, like trips to the pool hall or to shoot hoops in Ferndale. Or push-up competitions where we would just put a movie on and go back and forth doing push-ups until we couldn't lift our arms (I'm still the champ, D, and you know it). Or card games like "Dollar Tonk," which may sound pretty harmless, but you can lose your money real quick if you don't know what you're doing.

When an unsuspecting newcomer came over, I would get them with the "bread trick," betting that they couldn't eat two pieces of white bread in a minute without drinking water. They would always swear that they could perform the impossible feat, and I would always win back the money that I had lost in cards.

There I was, living on a different side of town than I was used to, living in an environment that I wasn't necessarily used to, and I took a step back, for a moment, long enough to see the smiles on the people's faces around me. Wal-Mart employees, welders, electricians, landscapers, people with their own car-detailing businesses—lots of people with their own car-detailing businesses. Maybe we were just "getting by," but most of us were doing our best to keep our spirits up, finding little bits of inspiration to keep us going. Our moving customers, surely, were thinking, "Could be worse. I could be moving furniture for a living." I was thinking, "Could be worse. I could be broke." The people that were broke were thinking, "Could be worse. I could be locked up." Not sure where the people in prison were getting their inspiration, though. Nevertheless, many of us in the free world had our sights set. Some of us had goals, plans for the future, and some of us didn't. Some of us wanted out and some of us were living day-to-day, paycheck-to-paycheck. But all of us were making an hourly wage and all of us were able to find our own level of happiness. A few of us, though, were able to maintain our discipline—distinguishing wants from needs and sacrificing what we wanted now for what we wanted later—while others couldn't. BG was struggling to find that discipline, but Derrick had it all figured out. He had known for quite some time what he wanted and in March, he got it.

He had been house hunting for about five months or so. He was participating in a non-profit organization called the Neighborhood Assistance Corporation of America (NACA), which helps make the dream of buying a home a reality for those with faulty credit or those who can't afford the closing costs and the ten percent that is usually required as a down payment. NACA walks its participants through the tedious process of purchasing their first house, a process that can typically be quite overwhelming for most people. Derrick went to every meeting and caught on quick. At the start, he didn't have a clue what he was doing. Five months later, he was quoting interest rates to me and showing me which neighborhoods were ripe for the picking in the real estate market.

I would say Derrick was about a year (eighteen months without a program like NACA) ahead of where I wanted to be. He had qualified for a house—his first true investment—and by the end of March, he was living in it. His very own (brand new!) home. Seventeen-hundred square feet, two stories, with a patio in the back for grilling and a fenced-in yard for his two-year-old daughter to play. No longer throwing his money away to a landlord, he had a tangible asset to his name. His monthly payments would build up equity in his house, and with the market looking like it was going to take a turn upward, who knows what its value would be in four or five years? Derrick had laid focus on the American Dream and there was no question that he was capturing it.

Considering the initial goals I had set forth before I began, my project had been finished on January 11, thirteen days shy of my six-month anniversary in Charleston. I had put away $2,514.36. Sure, rolling up the driver side window on my truck wasn't easy, and I used a flathead screwdriver in lieu of an ignition key, but it started. And, at the hands of the lone perk of my job as a mover, my apartment was furnished. I was done, complete, but, at the same time, I wasn't. I was just beginning. I wanted to see how far I could go. I had built a nice foundation, but there was so much more I could accomplish by July 24. There was no reason for me to turn back.

Why do I need to start drinking Dr. Pepper now, when I've been doing just fine with Dr. Thunder so far?

Is it really worth it for me—still "down here" in economic class— to shop at Lacoste and Eddie Bauer when I can look just as good in far less expensive clothes by shopping at the Goodwill or, when I get a good tip, Marshalls?

I was still always looking for ways to save money, always on the hunt for a deal. "Two for a buck? I'll take 'em!" I didn't care what it was. Pork and beans became a new food group to me just because it was always on sale at Food Lion. If the price was right, I could find a use for it. I was a scrooge, greedy. My money! Get your hands off. I'd worked hard, and I was surely going to see to it that I continued to be wise with what I earned. After all, is this really where I wanted to be? If nothing else, I had merely ascended *into* poverty—certainly not *out* of it—so I wanted to continue to save, making plans the whole time for what I would do with my loot. How I could invest it to make it so much more valuable to me? One can do a lot with $2,500, so I could only imagine the possibilities in July after I accumulated six more months of paychecks. Night classes at Trident Tech? My own moving truck? An entirely different trade altogether? That's what kept me going: the idea that I had a better lifestyle in sight. *I'm not moving furniture forever. I can promise you that.*

As the frost (yes, there is frost in South Carolina) began to subside, and spring blossomed, I was hitting a groove. Derrick was no longer our neighbor, which sucked big time, since he was my main source of entertainment, but I was getting my fill of him at work, and BG was doing more than his fair share of keeping things exciting at home.

With only four months left in my project, I could only imagine that I had reached the height of my experience in Charleston and that I would cruise through the summer lifting furniture, scaring girls with my dance moves, and continuing to save money in preparation for my future life plans. But I was wrong. Nothing I had done in my life had prepared me for April's cultural lesson.

FIFTEEN

FIGHTING FOR RESPECT

The month of March had flown by quicker than I thought it would, so I was prepared for the same thing in April. A little excitement or drama here and there, but nothing too out of the ordinary.

But then the differences between BG and I really began to surface.

He was getting on my nerves, and it was starting to become more and more serious as time passed. It was growing to be a bit more than a few wisecracks back and forth about each other's facial features. And usually it surrounded the use of my truck. I didn't mind feeding him once in a while or letting him borrow some laundry detergent. I didn't even mind when he borrowed my truck—"borrowed" being the operative word, implying that he would ask first and thereafter return my truck within the agreed upon time and in the same condition as it had been before. But that was rarely the case. He would take my truck and be gone for hours, unaware (or perhaps, indifferent) to the fact that maybe I would need to use it. Twice he even returned it with dings on the hood and once it came back with the front fender bent into a forty-five-degree angle as if he had run into a pole. Every time, though, he didn't have a legitimate answer for what had happened or why he had my truck for seven hours longer than we had agreed. "Shoot, it was like that when I left," he would say.

So, as time progressed, I saw the need to develop a few war tactics to maintain the security of my truck. My comments about having a little consideration when it came to borrowing my truck—the truck *I* fueled and insured, the truck *I* had bought—had fallen on deaf ears. BG was going to learn a lesson, and I was going to be his teacher.

The first eighteen or so times that he had been tardy on returning my truck, I had gone easy on him. "Don't do it again," I would say, and he would agree. But then it would happen again and again and again, and after the nineteenth time, I had had enough.

He had borrowed my truck at 7:00 PM to run to Auto Zone to pick up a new tail light since mine had burned out. Nice guy, right? At 10:30, he was still there. Unfortunately for him, I knew it was karaoke night at LD's, and since LD's was only about a mile from our house, I walked up there just to satisfy my own curiosity. And lo and behold, there it was, my little truck, an eyesore parked so innocently among some of the shiniest cars in Charleston.

So, I "stole" my truck from BG, drove it back home, and parked it around the corner where he wouldn't see it. He came home just after midnight, tired from walking, and woke me up from my pretense slumber on the couch.

"Adam, dog. Somebody done stole your truck, homie."

"What?" I asked, groggy-eyed. "What are you talking about?"

"Your truck. It was at LD's, but it ain't there no mo'."

"Jesus, BG. I thought you were just going up to Auto Zone. What the hell?"

"I know, man. I'm sorry. Karaoke night, you know."

"Oh, man. Karaoke night?" I wasn't happy, and he was getting a little nervous. "That's pretty interesting. But not my problem." I rolled back over to go back to sleep. "I don't care where it is. You took it.

Now, go find it."

So he walked back up to the LD's parking lot and back, to make sure it wasn't there. He had been quite intoxicated before, so he thought his eyes may have been playing tricks on him.

Nope.

"Shoot, man," he said when he returned nearly an hour later. "Everybody around knows you can start it with a screwdriver, so it was probably one of them." He started making phone calls. Bonesy. Vurt. Fonz. Rabbit. Nobody knew what he was talking about.

"Well, Shep," he said, finally apologetic. "I reckon we gonna have to call the police."

So I stopped him there and told him where the truck was. Happy that nobody had stolen it, he got the point that I was trying to make, that he needed to have a little more consideration for me and my truck. Whew. Case closed.

Until three days later, when he violated the privileges of using my truck. Again.

He had gone to Sheniya's house even though he told me he was running to Burger King to get some food. I knew he was there, because I heard him making plans ahead of time. "A'ight, I'll be over there in a minute, girl ... Hey, Shep! I'm taking the truck to grab a burger right quick. I'll be right back."

I didn't have anywhere to go or anything important to do, so I watched a movie and took a nap and prepared to exact my revenge. After he'd been gone four hours, I called him on Sheniya's phone. I knew how sensitive he was about the energy bill, so I played on what appeared to be his lone weakness.

"BG, check this out. Dog. I'm gonna tell you what's going on over here at four oh nine B Pine Hollow. Everything electrical in our house ... I'm turning it on. I'm talkin' everything. Lights, radios, TVs, microwave. Everything. I'm gonna go run the washing machine with no clothes in it. I'm gonna open the fridge door and keep it open, and I'm gonna turn on the garbage disposal in the sink. I might even borrow some appliances from the neighbors. It's gonna be like Chuck-E-Cheese's in here. When you come home with my truck, we'll turn everything off."

And then I hung up. I even turned the AC down to fifty degrees and opened all of the doors and windows. The electricity meter out back was spinning like a vinyl record, and I had a huge smile on my face. Sure, I had to pay half of the energy bill, too, but I was willing to fork over a few extra dollars for one more attempt at proving my point.

And he got it. He came rushing home and told me that he was sorry and that it wouldn't ever happen again.

Until four days later, in early April.

By this time, my tolerance was empty and so was my bag of tricks. I had run out of options, and I didn't know what to do. Refusing to allow him to borrow my truck was perhaps an option, but I really needed the tradeoff for his automotive skills to keep the truck operable.

It was just after four o'clock in the afternoon, BG had been gone with my truck for two hours, and I was growing antsy. It wasn't helping that I was watching a replay of Maury's "April Fooled! Is It a Woman or a Man?" and I had guessed wrong on an embarrassing six out of eight so far. BG was gone with my truck and he hadn't even lied to me about borrowing it by declaring that he had to run up the street real quick. He had simply taken it.

So I waited and waited, the temperature of my blood rising with every passing moment. My leg started shaking and I didn't even realize it. A hundred thoughts were running through my head, all surrounding how I was going to get BG to understand that he couldn't keep using my truck without permission.

When he came home and walked through the door, I just sat there, staring at him, deadpan, like a psychopath. Derrick was with him, right outside the front door, but I didn't know that at the time.

"Adam, listen, I know you're mad, but, check this out, I had to go pick Derrick up." He looked at Derrick. "Tell 'im."

Derrick stepped in the doorway. "It's true," he said, taking a sip of his drink. Evidently, they had made the detour by our house to give Derrick the opportunity to vouch for BG's character in the whole matter.

I just kept staring at BG. I didn't know what to say, but neither did he.

"I don't know what to tell you, dog. Somebody had to get 'im, and I was the only one available."

Staring, blood boiling. Later I would discover that he was lying anyway, that they had been shooting pool for the last couple of hours.

"Look, I know you're mad, Ad, but just don't even worry 'bout it. It ain't gonna happen again."

And that's when I got up and walked over to him. "You're damn right it won't happen again, mother fucker." Eloquently, I pronounced every syllable of every word slowly, with emphasis at the end. I grabbed his shirt by the chest and threw him up against the wall.

And that's when I realized exactly what I had done, what an idiot I was. I had known ahead of time that I wasn't a fighter, but for some reason, it just hadn't registered at that moment. Before that night with BG in early April, my record as a fighter stood at a disgraceful one and four, and that was in my neighborhood, the suburbs—Heather Hills—home of some of the worst fighters in the history of fighting. We were such bad fighters that people actually got bored watching us fight at school. "Eh, this sucks. Let's go back to class." And I was a particularly poor fighter. Even my one win had come from one lucky, sneaky punch, but none of that was clicking in my mind that night with BG. I was just really, really mad. That's all. My other efforts thus far had been in vain, and I didn't know any other way to get my point across to him.

But BG had other things on his mind, like whooping my sweet ass. I swear I think I saw his eyes light up after I grabbed him, like, "Oh, hell yeah. That's what I'm talkin' about, baby! Let's do this!"

So we did. In less than five seconds, he had stuck his leg behind mine and tripped me down onto my back. From there, it was all downhill for me. He put his left hand around my neck and just started wailing on me with his right. Remaining neutral, Derrick jumped in to try to break it up. He didn't care about motive or who had started it; he just wanted us to stop.

But BG wasn't stopping. He would have gone all night long, especially since he had the upper hand. The Brazilian Jiu-Jitsu techniques I had picked up watching Ultimate Fighting on TV were not working like I had planned. I was no match for BG, and I knew it before he even started swinging on me. Fighting was a sport for him. That is how he had grown up. He and his friends would beat the hell out of each other in the afternoon and then have sleepovers that same night. BG had grown up settling disputes with his knuckles whereas I had grown up talking things out or seeking creative means of revenge. Fighting? We might wrestle a little if things got really, really, really serious, but that was a rare occasion.

That night, though, BG didn't care much about our histories. He was completely immersed in the present. Thankfully, just as he was getting warmed up, Derrick finally peeled him off of me and sent him out the back door.

"Go outside! Go! Get the hell outta here, BG! Goddamn. You're gonna kill 'im!"

As much as I could exaggerate about the blood on the ground, I don't need to. It was everywhere—puddles of it, literally, on the ground, and splotches all over the walls. And unless he cut open one of his knuckles on a blow to my face, none of it was BG's. Most of it had come from my first fall to the ground when the back of my head had hit the corner of the windowsill in the front foyer and split open. The knockout blow. It didn't help matters that I was an over-bleeder, either, probably a hemophiliac. Little cuts had always needed an embarrassing number of bandages when I was growing up or the blood would have just kept coming, so you can imagine the effects of a deep gash. Later, BG told me that he thought Derrick's fruit punch had exploded all over the ground.

So, there I was, standing idle, right outside my front door, looking directly into the eyes of Derrick Hale, my hero, blood dripping down my neck. I was panting, gasping for breath like I was the one that had just gotten the workout.

"Damn, man," Derrick said. "What the hell was that? You ain't have to fight 'im. I understand where you're comin' from, but damn, you ain't have to fight 'im."

I looked down at all the blood on the ground and on my shirt. I touched my forehead and felt a bump. I licked my bottom lip and tasted blood. I took a second to ponder what had just happened.

To hell with this.

So I dodged Derrick and ran back through the house where BG was unlocking the door to get out. And I jumped on him. With all fours. If you're still trying to measure my fighting capabilities, there you go. I fight like a monkey.

Once again, he flipped me over and started pounding me. Derrick wasn't going to be so kind this time, though. He ran through the house, unclasping his jewelry along the way. "Y'all muh' fuckas gonna make me start swinging on both of y'all," he declared. His eyes were lighting up just like BG's had when I pushed him.

I don't know if BG was taking it easy on me on round two or not, but he didn't come at me as hard. I think he saw the blood spilling out of my head and onto the kitchen floor and walls and probably felt bad. Wow. He felt bad, so he took it easy on me. I had really wanted to teach him a lesson that night, teach him that my truck was *my* truck, but the tables had turned dramatically away from my favor. I would love to tell you that I underestimated him because of his indolent moving abilities, that his lethargic attitude shifted the odds in my favor, or that the last couple of months spent weightlifting and doing push ups played to my advantage. Nope. None of the above. It was David versus Goliath except we were about the same size and

BG didn't stop after the knockout blow. So, nothing like David versus Goliath, actually. More like Cain going after Abel, but I lived to tell the story.

And the entire debacle had been in slow motion, too. At least my end. People that get in fights will tell you, as they reminisce, "Man, I'm not sure exactly what happened. It was all such a blur to me." Ha. Not me. My fight with BG was in slow motion, like *The Matrix*. I remember everything, blow for blow. I remember it like a dream, a nightmare, where I was almost incapable of fighting back, as if my arms were being held back by some invisible force.

But it wasn't a dream, it wasn't slow motion, and my arms weren't being held back. It was real, fast, and I was just a lousy fighter.

In the end, after I cleaned the blood off the ground and touched up the walls with paint—both tasks that I performed within an hour after the fight—my biggest injury was the back of my head, which surely required stitches, but I refused to give BG the satisfaction of telling his friends that he had sent his pansy roommate to the hospital. I showered and walked around with a towel for the next two days until the gash stopped leaking.

Later that night, Derrick called to make sure I was all right, relaying the message from BG that I had more fight in me than anybody else he'd whooped on in the past. I took that as the compliment it was meant to be, although it was surely an exaggeration, especially considering the fact that I got in maybe half of a blow. Later BG refined his comment by telling me that I was one of the elite class of his victims that had come back for a second round.

BG spent the night at Derrick's, and we didn't talk for three days. When we finally did break the silence, we both apologized—me for throwing him against the wall and him for pummeling me like he did. And then he apologized for stealing my truck all of the time. "I didn't really know it was that serious to you," he told me.

In any event, it was incredible how my relationship with BG grew from there. We were like best friends. He asked me before he borrowed my truck, and he started returning within the time limits I set. He even started taking out the trash on a regular basis and buying groceries. Once, he brought home a pizza for us to share. No toppings, but it was the gesture that counted. Maybe he was just feeling bad for what he had done to me, but I didn't care. We both had learned a lesson or two, and, as a result, we had a little more compassion working for us.

Maybe the change came since we decided it wouldn't be a good idea for us to work together anymore at Fast Company. Working and living together was taking its toll and we knew it. So he went to work for another crew, leaving Derrick and I with a different guy every day.

So that was it! By the middle of April, BG and I were building the foundation for a brand-new relationship and we were rolling. He was giving his paychecks to Derrick (his bank) and I was continuing to save money, too. BG was even on the hunt for a second job. (He inquired at LD's about being a bouncer, but they laughed at him. "Be serious, B. *You*? A bouncer? Ha!")

As the season continued to roll toward warmer months, we were loving life, all of us, together, taking on the world. But just as my friendships really began to blossom, my time in Charleston reached its abrupt and unexpected conclusion.

SIXTEEN

ONE LAST MOVE

❦

My parents' health was the main reason that I had restricted my project to the Southeast rather than heading out west to Texas or Colorado or California, or up north to Wisconsin or Pennsylvania. Both of them had cancer (my mom, lymphoma, and my dad, prostate cancer) when I had left in July, and I wanted to be close in the event of an emergency. Lymphoma, when caught early, is generally not one of the more serious forms of cancer, however, Mom had a very rare T-cell lymphoma, which turned out to be quite aggressive. And the chemotherapy took its toll. Her hair was gone and her energy was drained, but her will was unscathed. Luckily, they had caught Mom's cancer early enough, so it was treated before it had the opportunity to spread away from her lymph nodes. By December, six months after the onset of the disease, she had gone through the necessary treatments and the cancer was in remission. My pops—armed with a new diet and workout routine—also had his situation well under control. Even though I had to follow their situations from afar, things were looking up.

But then, in March, my mom's cancer returned and with even greater aggression. Mom would have to go through high-dose chemotherapy treatments (twice, since the first one would be interrupted by a series of infections that needed to be treated with antibiotics in the hospital) and then she would have to go through a very intense stem-cell transplant. After all of that came the tough part, the recovery process, which was said to be just as difficult as the actual treatment, since it was anticipated to be long and tedious.

My mom is a fighter, with a vibrant spirit at every battle. She's never really asked for anything from anybody. She is always giving, always looking out for the interests of others. When I was in high school, my friends didn't come to my basketball games to see me play; they came to hang out with my mom. She's that kind of person. And for the first time in her life, she needed help, support from those who loved her most.

Nothing in my life had prepared me for her sickness the first go around, where she fought through the treatments like a champ, so you can imagine how taken aback we all were when the cancer returned. Joanie Shepard—a woman filled with optimism and spirit, the most independent person in the world—actually needed assistance. It was a new situation to me. It was the first time in my life that I had ever witnessed someone close to me suffering. My Uncle Donald, who had passed away in January during my time in Charleston, was perhaps the lone exception, but even he had died with a smile on his face after eighty-four fruitful years of living.

Mom had a job prior to her lymphoma, but the unemployment benefits ran out during the first round of treatments. With the second round, finances were going to be tight. My father and brother lived in Raleigh and were able to look after her—running errands, taxiing her to and from the hospital for tests and treatments, and the like—but my parents were divorced, so my mom didn't have a crutch to lean on for financial support. The only thing standing between her and broke was a meager disability check and an even more laughable savings account.

That's where I came in, perhaps the ultimate irony of my entire project. With each of us working hard enough just to support ourselves, my brother Erik and I had to come together to provide financial support for our mom. I was to head home to Raleigh, where Erik and I would split the costs on a three-bedroom apartment to look after my mom, to essentially do what I was doing in Charleston, except now it was for real, beyond the scope of my project. I was being called home to Raleigh, where I would work for the local branch of Fast Company and then as a wheelchair attendant at the airport for as long as it took for my mom to become self-sufficient and ready to go on with her life as her own, new person. When she was better, I would head to New York or California where I would have the freedom to begin to use my college degree in search of my own passion.

My professional plans were put on the back burner as I had more important business to tend to. Unfortunately, I would have to start over on the bottom rung at the Fast Company in Raleigh. Each franchise is independently owned and operated, so, while it would be rather easy for me to get a job there based on my experience, my salary would not transfer. By April, I had worked my way up to $11 an hour at the Fast Company in Charleston, but in Raleigh, I would start over and have to prove my worth to the company once again.

At the end of April, with my time at Fast Company in Charleston coming to an end, I began thinking about how well I had done, how I had stacked up as a worker. Was I average or above or below? How would my peers grade my moving abilities?

I figured many of the guys at the shop would probably give me a "C," since most of them hadn't had the opportunity to work with me for longer than a day or two, and since they mostly knew me by my catch-me shorts and horrendous truck-packing abilities. (Of the three times that Derrick had me pack the truck on small moves, he had to take over twice after seeing that we weren't going to be able to make it on one trip. The other time, we drove to the unload with the back doors open and a dog house strapped over the edge.)

The management (Pam and Chris) would most certainly give me an "A" since they didn't care if I was an efficient mover or not. As long as I was coming into the shop in the morning ready to work and in uniform and returning in the evening without a damage report, I was gold to them.

The customers would also rate me pretty high, I think, but there again, the grading scale was pretty slack. They would give high marks to any one of the guys at Fast Company who were delivering their furniture from one house to the next without a scratch on it. The customers couldn't tell if we were fast or slow. By their standards, every mover was fast.

On the other hand, Derrick's rating of my moving skills was a tricky guess. He would surely tell his buddies that I was a "D-minus," just to be a badass, but with extra credit for my improvement as a reckless driver over the months, he would probably consider me to be about a "B."

A "B." Yep, that's probably what I was, if that. I was average—not terribly strong, not terribly quick, not terribly knowledgeable. All I had going for me, really, was my ability to listen and my stamina, the fact that I could work all day with only a jug of water and a bag of trail mix as fuel. Derrick brought the best out of me, no doubt, but even then, I still couldn't hang with him. I was just another guy in the shop, fighting to make a living while dragging behind Fast Company's finest.

I packed my belongings on the last Sunday in April and prepared to leave Charleston. I thought about what I had done, what I had accomplished, and the challenges to come. I was not, by any means, looking forward to moving furniture in Raleigh. One, perhaps, would have imagined that after my nine months in South Carolina I would have grown used to the difficulties of moving furniture every day, unaffected by the tediousness of the job and the sore muscles and joints that followed in the evening. But that wasn't the case at all. It had been incredibly demanding on my body, increasingly so with each passing day. My back would burn in the morning when I woke up, and my legs would follow suit in the afternoon. There was no immunity to it, no moment when things would "click" and my body's defense mechanisms would ward off the aches and pains of bending and lifting. At least if there was, it hadn't happened to me yet.

So there I was, the bed of my pickup truck packed with boxes of toiletries and wall decorations and lamps and bags of linens and clothes, ready to hit the road to begin life anew, again, with new people and challenges to meet and new ambitions to pursue. While paying monthly expenses and buying food and fuel and funding my own social agenda, my bank account and cash on hand totaled just under $5,300 from wages and tips, more than enough to finance whatever my next dream would be. I was pumped. I looked at what I had done, and I looked at what I had experienced. From my first night on the streets of Charleston to living in the shelter to working with Shaun at Fast Company and then finally working my way up to join Derrick's crew and live with BG, I was proud of what I had accomplished. But, in truth, I really looked forward to tomorrow. In the future, no matter where I stood financially, I could rest easy knowing that things were going to be OK. *Look at what I've done with $25. Imagine what I can do with $5,000 and the money that I'll continue to earn as I complete my project.*

I knew the coming months wouldn't be easy, but I was happy to be able to care for my mom, no matter where my financial situation stood.

I knew that Derrick's future was bright. I didn't have to see his beautiful house or his whopping bank account to know that. He had that killer instinct, the hardworking aura emitting from him that showed that he was ready to meet, head-on, any challenge that stood in his way.

The last time I saw Derrick was the Saturday night before I left for Raleigh. He was having a belated housewarming party, and he invited a few people over for food and drinks. In his world, a "few people" could easily turn in to busloads, which it did. As soon as word got out around Kingstree that Derrick Hale was having a party back in Charleston (free food and drinks everybody!), his house was full of people. For me, it was uneventful, not exactly my scene. I showed up, had a hot dog, and talked with his wife. Derrick was preoccupied in the garage, shooting dice with his friends. He shook my hand in passing to the bathroom but quickly returned to his game. I left the party shortly thereafter, a very undramatic exit.

After I got back to Raleigh, Derrick and I would exchange stories of our moving woes over the phone. Working without Derrick, even for just a short time, would turn out to be one of the more difficult experiences of my life. Aside from the emotional drain of dealing with my mom's illness, I had to work with a different Fast Company crew every day—guys that didn't have half of the expertise or work ethic as the movers in Charleston but, interestingly, were still getting paid over $1.50 more per hour. Forget moving with Derrick. I was spoiled rotten having had that opportunity. That summer in Raleigh before I moved on to work as a wheelchair attendant at the airport, I even grew to appreciate, and miss, the days moving with BG.

I was pulling for BG, but I couldn't be certain what the future held for him. Fifty dollars at a time, he had nearly emptied the account he had been keeping with Derrick and was back to squeaking by, paycheck-to-paycheck. If nothing else, his expenses, though, were declining since he was filling my vacant spot with two other guys. After hearing that I was leaving, he had put the word out among his cronies that he needed a new roommate until our lease was up in December, and in just a short time he had received a huge response from people that wanted to move in. So, he picked the two closest to him (Vurt and Jaime) to move in and split all of the expenses three ways instead of two. Vurt would sleep on the couch and Jaime would sleep in my old room. Jaime had been living at a hotel, so I sold all of my furniture to him for $80, which turned out to be a sweet deal for both of us. I didn't have to haul it home, and he would have a little something to begin his own new life, a jump start, just like Crisis Ministries had given me at the beginning of my journey.

On that final Sunday, though, before I hit the road with everything I owned riding along with me, I had one last stop to make: Mama D's Dirty South Barbecue. I couldn't resist one final trip there, but I also wanted to take BG out to lunch and tell him who I really was. My "outing" to Derrick three days prior had been met with unemotional indifference. After all, I was modeling my project after a lifestyle in which he had already proven successful, so, if anything, I had been learning from him.

Unfortunately, after BG and I packed the truck, there was no room in the front seat for him to fit, so we exchanged our last good-byes outside in the driveway. Leaning on the bed of my truck, I took the time to explain to BG how I had come to arrive in Charleston, what my project had been all about. I explained that I had started with virtually nothing and was now heading back to Raleigh with, well, something. We discussed how I had done it—with thrifty spending and aggressive saving—and I told him that he was ahead of where I was when I started. With a little patience and discipline, he could accomplish the same things that I had accomplished. I told him that if he wanted out of this lifestyle, he could get there; it all started with a little goal setting and a few budgeting techniques and then it would sprout from there. I told him that it would be a shame for him to be scraping by for the rest of his life when he had the potential—I know it—to do so much better.

The conversation was two-sided and never disrespectful either way. He admitted that he had made some questionable decisions with his social life and that he could probably tighten up in some areas.

He told me that he knew what he had been doing was wrong and he knew what he had to do to change direction. He loved his friends, he said, but he knew that their up-to-no-good influence was wearing on him.

I told him I believed in him and that I was going to miss him and his exciting, mischievous behavior. I told him to be good to all of his girls.

And then I shook his hand, hopped in my truck, stuck the screwdriver in the ignition, and drove toward the next step in my life.

A YEAR LATER:

A DIDACTIC LOOK AT WHAT I LEARNED AND WHERE WE GO FROM HERE

o there it is. My 365-day climb from nothing to something; my 365-day experience in a culture that I had only observed from afar prior to living in Charleston.

I want to say that my year flew by as quickly as I have written, but that wasn't the case at all. Nearly every day seemed to meander by in slow motion. I could have written another hundred pages filled with war stories from the guys at the shelter: stories about the guy who got stabbed outside the shelter with a six-inch blade and came to the soup kitchen the next day showing off his wound; stories about the move where we had to dodge dog bombs throughout the entire house; stories about the move where the customer backed into the mailbox, pulled forward, and got out, again leaving his car in reverse and sending it back into the mailbox; stories about out-of-town moves to Florida and Virginia and the side move where I accompanied Brooklyn Bonesy (a narcoleptic pothead) to Tennessee; more woes and good times with BG; the crack-ring bust in our neighborhood. And the list goes on.

If you had asked me in July of 2006 what I had the potential to accomplish during this project, I would have told you what I thought I could do, but indeed, in the end, I exceeded my own expectations. I had no idea what to expect in Charleston, and I must say it was quite a learning experience. When I began, I could never have guessed that I would have the experiences that I had or meet the people that I did. I didn't imagine that homeless shelters like Crisis Ministries offered the services that they do, and I certainly didn't imagine that guys like Omar and Phil Coleman and Easy E and "Hustle Man" even existed in those shelters. I had assumed that everybody would be old, hairy, and smelly.

And later, outside of the shelter, I had no idea that guys like Derrick and BG, having come from the same rural hometown with limited opportunity, could have such different attitudes about life. Although I speculated, I never would have imagined that the cultural differences between BG and I would lead to such drama, and I certainly had no idea that my time in Charleston would end so abruptly. I was clueless.

But, in the end, what did I really learn about the vitality of the American Dream? What conclusions am I able to draw on the persistence of poverty in America? What am I able to take away from my experience within an entirely different culture than the one where I was raised? And most importantly, where do we go from here?

For starters, I learned that we are the product of our surroundings—our families, our peers, and our environment. If a child grows up among poor attitudes, zero ambition, and parents that say, "I ain't got no sugar," then he or she is probably going to one day have a poor attitude, zero ambition, and is going to say, "I ain't got no sugar." Many break out, of course. There are countless stories of

PhDs and corporate executives and attorneys that have broken free from the reins of the lower classes in spite of their humble beginnings. It happens all of the time, but the odds are most certainly stacked against them. I consider myself even more fortunate now than when I began my project: my parents are educated and loving and they showed me the way. Now, more than ever, I understand that things could have been much different for me in my life. I was lucky. Some are not.

I learned that life is a bitch. Everybody faces adversity. *Everybody.* Nobody is immune. I met—and lived alongside—poor people in Charleston who were miserable and others who were delighted with their lives. By the same token, I've met millionaires in my life who have found true happiness just as I have met millionaires who are some of the least happy people on the planet simply because they don't know how to handle their wealth or, worse, they have never even had the opportunity to discover what happiness is in the first place. Adversity attacks every level.

Yeah, life is a bitch for sure. Or actually, let me rephrase that: life *can be* a bitch. It's all about how we look at things. Moving furniture sucks. Breaking your toe or suffering through seven days of diarrhea sucks. I would have loved a day off, time to relax and rest, maybe a vacation. But that is unrealistic. Good times abound, but time off is a poor investment if you live at the bottom. There are plenty of ways to have fun, plenty of ways to look at our lives as more than just tolerable. All the while, we have to be more focused, keeping our eye on what we really want to do with our lives: move up. Or not. We're either on a mission or keeping our flight grounded. Either way, *we* are the pilots.

More than anything else over the course of my project, I grew to appreciate, even more than before, that we live in the greatest country in the world. America is more fertile and full of more opportunity than any other country. We are the eminent superpower of the planet. Can you imagine the results if I would have done my project anywhere else in the world? You think I would have had quite the success if I would have started in Asia or Eastern Europe or Latin America? You ever been to Guatemala? Wow. You want to talk about poor people with little opportunity? They live in huts, grow their own food, and drink unsanitary water. Their economy is so bad that they immigrate to Mexico in search of more favorable circumstances. So, in spite of all the whining and complaining that goes on in our country, I'd say we're doing all right.

Perhaps the ultimate irony of my project is that the American Dream has evolved into so much more than financial ambition. It used to be that a European sold all of his possessions and sailed to Ellis Island with $100 in his back pocket and a dream in his head. He worked hard in a factory, got married, and had 2.3 kids. His children worked hard and got an education so that their children could have a better life. And on and on and on and well, here we are.

But today, the American Dream means so much more. Coupled with the ideal that you have the freedom to work hard and accomplish what you want in your life, it's about finding happiness and solace in your present lifestyle. This is a fact. I know it, because I saw it. Just as I met people that would rather own a Cadillac with shiny chrome rims than a home, I met people who didn't care about their car or their furnishings or where they lived; they knew they'd have all of that one day, and they were driven by that satisfaction and that motivation. Some are happy now and are on a quest to stay that way. Others, in search of unworthy pursuits, are after a happiness that they may never find.

Why? Mainly, because so many of us don't have five-year plans on how we are going to better our lot over time rather than search for quick fixes. A five-year plan is invaluable. It gives us a sense of purpose in our present lives, the peace of mind every day that what we are doing has a purpose, a means to an end. A five-year plan doesn't have to be set in stone, but rather should be an amendable draft that serves as a guideline for our future. A fat savings account, a house, a business, a management position. Knowing what we want and setting the gears in motion gets us up in the morning and keeps us going throughout the day. "In five years, I'm going to be doing bigger and better things." Exactly. Now, go do it. (I'm not bitter. Some people do have five-year plans. I met a guy when I was working at RDU Airport who went grocery shopping every two weeks at BJ's Warehouse and bought all of his food for that time period. He never went out to eat, always packed his meals, or cooked them at home. Why? "I did a little experiment a few years ago," he said. "My wife and I save six hundred dollars a month this way.")

Unfortunately, few of us take ownership of our lives. We live in an "It ain't my fault" society. Nothing is our fault. Ever. We're fat because of our genetics, we suck at math because we had a bad teacher, and we're cheating on our wives because they aren't putting out like they used to. It has nothing to do with the fact that we aren't eating right or exercising, that we aren't doing our homework, or that we aren't pulling our own weight in our marriages. It's everybody else's fault. It ain't ours.

And that's the biggest difference I noticed between the people who appeared happy and those who didn't—those who I could tell were working their way up, like Derrick, and those that were "lifers," like Shaun. Derrick knew what he had to do and he didn't make excuses to cover his mistakes. Shaun, always the victim, walked around like somebody owed him something.

It's a pretty simple concept, actually: one day, you're twenty and full of potential, and the next day you're eighty, submerged in a world of reminiscence. Are you proud of those last sixty years or are you looking back with a chip on your shoulder, mad that you *could have* done a little more?

The bottom line is that we have a lot of work to do. Attitudes need to change, big time, on both fronts. Both sides and in the middle. The livelihood of the poor is at stake just as is the livelihood of the higher ups. We're only as strong as our weakest link, right?

In the end, though, where do we turn for help? Whose responsibility is it to offer assistance to those in need?

Well, everybody's.

I've already made an attempt at pointing out that those at the bottom can work harder to do their part. Pull yourself up by your bootstraps. There's nothing revolutionary about that aspect of my story. That's just life. Some people get it done; others don't. Some people merely have a dream, while others have a vision of turning that dream into reality. Some people put ten percent of their paycheck in the bank and others buy lottery tickets and beer. (I read a story recently about a guy that went to a financial advisor with $42 when he was twenty-eight. "I don't know what to do with this money," he said. "But I want you to show me." He saved all of his extra money every month, and thirty years later, he retired as a millionaire.)

But what about everybody else? What about government programs? Surely, current welfare programs just aren't cutting it, but what is the alternative?

To begin with, we need to acknowledge that our system is flawed and that we can be doing better. There isn't one fix-all answer out there, but there are steps that we can take to begin to appease the cycle of poverty. A friend of mine from Ohio—Neil Cotiaux—offered me those steps:

1) More free classes on parenting skills are needed to help create a better environment for at-risk infants and young people.
2) The government must step up its commitment to clean, safe, affordable housing in new and innovative ways. Too much is spent on defense and not enough on domestic programs. Affordable housing needs additional support from both the legislative and executive branches at the federal and state levels. Home ownership education programs for first-time home buyers appear in good supply, but the stock of accessible housing needs work.
3) Free financial literacy instruction in the vernacular of the street

or in immigrants' native tongue must be widely offered. Stock market board games sponsored by local companies in high schools sound nice but don't address the proper issues—needs versus wants, saving versus spending, developing a budget, etc.

4) Reading is a core foundation. "Reading aloud" and reading instruction at the preschool level is essential. It helps develop a core competency, and it (hopefully) demonstrates that someone cares.

5) Customized bundles of social services delivered by a local coalition of volunteers, nonprofits, and for-profits should be increasingly built into new housing supply. Bring parenting, financial literacy, housing maintenance, and other skills to at-risk individuals and families where they live. Gather a (somewhat) captive audience in familiar, non-threatening surroundings.

6) Reform school funding formulas to make the caliber of instruction more equitable across districts.

7) Place the snowballing cry for universal access to college education in the proper perspective. Where should finite government resources go—to support vulnerable children getting started in life or to those more ready to enter the halls of ivy? Fund the sons and daughters of the working poor first, and let them find their way. They may find their way through JobCorps, an apprenticeship, the military, or some other route; or perhaps college.

These are not aggressive policy changes that will require massive funding. But even if taxes do go up, isn't that a small price to pay if we can feel confident that we are subsidizing legitimate programs that offer a hand up to the poor rather than a hand out? A hike in minimum wage is fun to talk about, but, in the end, economically speaking, it isn't a worthy option. Higher wages mean higher costs, which mean higher prices across the board. With a $10 minimum wage, the ninety-nine-cent value menu at Wendy's becomes the $1.99 value menu, and so on, so what's the point? If $7 an hour isn't supporting your current lifestyle, then you have other options: A) team up with a friend or family member to help cover living expenses, B) change your lifestyle, or C) use that job as the stepping stone it is meant to be in your quest for better opportunities.

With all of this said, it is important that I acknowledge that poverty will be around forever. I don't say this as a downer, but rather as a simple reality. While I have more sympathy for the poor now than when I started, I also understand that poverty is going to be around for reasons beyond a person's unlucky childhood. Even after countless lessons learned, some people will always find it easier to remain apathetic and make bad decisions, to lie down rather than getting up to fight.

To a certain extent, I am able to forgive youngsters who have grown up in substandard conditions and subsequently made poor decisions. The young girl who spread her legs and pooped out two kids before finishing high school? Maybe that's all she knew growing up. Nobody was in her ear, daily, deterring her from making poor decisions. Role models? Ha! They were making the same bad decisions. Now, at age 28, she has two choices: A) maintain her present status or B) recognize her mistakes and head on the road to create a better life for herself and her children. We are rewarded for good decisions and dealt a lesson for bad ones. Just as we have to live with the joys of having children, for example, we have to live with the financial setbacks. Wendy from Fast Company got pregnant at nineteen, a decision she wouldn't change if she could. Now a thirty-one-year-old single mother, she is kicking right along—living in a trailer and keeping a close eye on her daughter's future. She doesn't spend her paycheck on beer and cigarettes and other such luxuries. She saves. Her back is against the wall, but her sights are set on tomorrow. "I can promise you my daughter's going to college," she told me.

I am unable, however, to excuse the repetition of the same

mistakes: the twenty-five-year-old adults smoking and drinking and chasing women or the deadbeats sitting at home, in poverty, watching a movie on their big-screen TV, waiting to scratch off the winning lotto numbers. (I met a guy once on the bus who spent several minutes telling me his method of picking a winning scratch lottery ticket. "There's a science to it," he told me. "And I know that science.") Because that's all they know? It's time to grow up. Do you really want to live like that forever? Many have given up, refusing to work hard, and, as I said, I am unable to show sympathy for them.

The ever-present war between liberals and conservatives on the causes, effects, and solutions to poverty will be debated forever. Good. Let 'em fight it out. But what about us, the rest of us, who don't have a voice in government or who are waiting for our policy proposals to be debated? Is there anything we can do?

Um, yeah, there is.

Imagine if we could reach out to the underprivileged. One out of four, two out of five, one out of ten—whatever. I say that's more of a success than sitting back and saying, "Welp, poverty isn't goin' anywhere" or "Um, I'm doing my part: I pay taxes." Give me a break. You can do better than that. You! You can do something. Forget the government for a moment. *You* have the opportunity to make a small contribution and become a part of something big. Pick up the phone and volunteer, caution a parent on his or her questionable behavior, make a forgivable loan. Better yet, go down to your local elementary or middle school and volunteer for two, three hours a week after school. Read to a child, help him or her with fractions. Teach him or her how to play tennis. Take him or her to the movies. Both my Resident Director from Merrimack and my pops participate in mentoring programs similar to the Big Brothers Big Sisters program, and they swear it has been one of the most rewarding experiences of their lives. To take a child to the zoo or to the aquarium—places he or she has never been; to make a difference in these young people's lives; to give them the assistance that they are not getting at home

... You can't buy happiness like that, and the government surely can't afford to fund it.

One of the most popular programs at my college was Alternative Spring Break. Rather than spending the second week of March sipping on margaritas and bronzing their skins on the beaches of Miami or Jamaica or Cancun, students headed to places like Philadelphia or Chicago or the Bronx where they picked up a hammer and built a house for a needy family. And on their own dime, too. So, don't tell me that we don't care. Please. Americans care. Programs like ASB flourish. Maybe we underestimate ourselves, but—one at a time—we do care.

Which reminds me ... we need more heroes. Boy, do we need more heroes. Ken Griffey Jr. is a hero as are Larry Bird, Dr. Martin Luther King Jr., Ellen, and Oprah, but that's not what I'm talking about. We need more neighborhood heroes, more small timers stepping up against the crowd to show what it takes to embrace change. I hate to keep bringing him up, but Derrick is the perfect example. He is my hero. There's a reason why he rose from the pits of poverty and made it out while others haven't—hard work, discipline, a good attitude, smart decisions. It doesn't happen if you sit on your front stoop sipping on a can of Natural Light, and it doesn't happen if you are reckless with your hard-earned money.

And do you think BG looks up to Derrick? You're damn right he does. Guys like BG, who never had anyone to look up to, have no other choice but to look to their peers for guidance. Can you imagine the effects if we had more guys like Derrick as role models? Guys with their mouths shut, walking the walk, *showing* what it takes to avoid being another statistic. Wow. It could become contagious. It would be like a real-life multi-level marketing scheme.

I was at the airport once, and a guy really put this attitude into perspective for me. We were at the baggage claim, standing back, watching everyone attack the front of the conveyor belt to retrieve their bags. "Look at this," he said. "Look at these people. They're all so hungry to fetch their own two big bags of luggage, but nobody cares about that little old lady over there who is struggling with just her one. Ha. That's life for ya."

There it is. Life is a baggage claim.

You can say what you want about my project, how it was flawed because of this or that. What if I had picked Jacksonville or Mobile or Savannah out of the hat instead of Charleston? And what if I would have had kids to tow around or what if I wouldn't have struck the luck that I did in working with the greatest mover on the planet? Fair enough, but I've heard it all from the people who have critiqued my book along the way. I hope, though, that those criticisms of this book don't take away from the fact that my story is by no means unique. The point stands that we can do something about our plight or not. It is what it is. Get out and do something. After all, what is the alternative? Scrape by forever, complaining the whole time about how we've been done wrong? Oh, poor us. I'm telling you, it doesn't have to be that way.

So, here I go, to retreat into my white-collar world, armed with my college education and the personal belongings that I have acquired over the last year. But let's be honest here. Excluding my college education, is my life really that different now? I'm going to use the same spending and savings tactics that I used in Charleston. I'm going to continue to eat Rice-A-Roni and buy shirts for $10 and search for cheap entertainment. I'll seek inexpensive transportation until, perhaps one day, I'm independently wealthy and I can afford a nicer car. And you better believe that a series of corporate executives are going to get the same speech that I gave to Curtis at Fast Company. I won't stop until one of those guys hires me on to fetch him coffee in exchange for his expertise and the opportunity to climb into the ranks of management. I'll work my way up that infamous corporate ladder or perhaps go into business for myself, hopefully finding something that I am passionate about along the way.

That's how it's supposed to be. A blank canvas and unlimited upside potential. It's the foundation of the American Dream.

In chapter eight, toward the end of my stay at Crisis Ministries, Leo told me what he thought the three types of people are in our world. My friend Surry offered me his version:

1) Those who make things happen;
2) Those who watch things happen;
3) Those who sit back, scratch their heads, and wonder, "What in the hell just happened?"

There it is. Three choices. Reread that and think about it for a second. One, two, or three. Three choices. That's it!

Which one are you?

ABOUT THE AUTHOR

Adam Shepard is a 2006 graduate of Merrimack College in North Andover, MA where he majored in Business Management and Spanish. Serving as a Resident Advisor during his upperclassmen years, he began to take particular interest in the social issues of our nation. Shortly after graduation—with almost literally $25 to his name—Shepard departed his home state for Charleston, SC, embarking on the journey that has now become *Scratch Beginnings*.

Scratch Beginnings is Shepard's first work. He presently lives in Raleigh, North Carolina with his mom.

For more information, including a Practical Reading
Guide for Teachers and Reading Groups, visit:

www.scratchbeginnings.com